FROST IN
FLORIDA

FROST IN FLORIDA

A Memoir

HELEN MUIR

Valiant Press

Valiant Press, Inc.
P.O. Box 330568, Miami, FL 33233

© 1995 by Helen Muir
All rights reserved. Published 1995
Printed in the United States of America
00 99 98 97 96 95 5 4 3 2 1
Designed by Gwyn J. Allison

Permissions to use photographs and copyrighted material have been generously granted by individuals and
publishers. Acknowledgment can be found under Permissions at the back of this book.

Library of Congress Cataloging-in-Publication Data

Muir, Helen, 1911-
    Frost in Florida : a memoir / Helen Muir.
      p.   cm.
    Includes bibliographical references and index
    ISBN 0-9633461-6-4
    1. Frost, Robert. 1874-1963—Homes and haunts—
Florida—Miami. 2. Poets, American—20th century—
Biography. 3. Frost, Robert, 1874-1963—Friends and
associates. 4. Muir, Helen, 1911- —Friends and asso-
ciates. 5. Literary landmarks—Florida—Miami. 6.
Florida—Intellectual life—20th century. I. Title.
PS3511.R94Z799 1995
811'.52—dc20
  [B]   95-13167
                                                CIP

"What is memory but the repository of things doomed to be forgotten, so you must have History. You must labor to invent History. Being faithful to all that happens to you of significance, recording days, dates, events, names, sights not relying merely upon memory which fades like a Polaroid print where you see the memory fading before your eyes like time itself retreating."

—Joyce Carol Oates

CONTENTS

INTRODUCTION

In the summer of 1994 an advertisement appeared in *The Miami Herald* with a photograph depicting a large two-story Key West-type residence with a glimpse of the roof of a smaller building showing very close by. It read like this: "DAVIS PONCE RD AREA Wonderful Florida native design w/wraparound verandahs, hrdwd flring, French drs, 7br, 7bths, 2 historic Robert Frost cottages."

The publisher of this book, Charity Johnson, caught this gobbledygook message and nothing would do but that we arrange to go view the Frost cottages, now receiving second-billing status.

It had been more than thirty years since I had sat and listened to Robert Frost read Browning and Longfellow to my husband and me in one of those little houses. I often had lunch in the kitchen alone with Frost and once, a year before his death, it was necessary for me to sleep there when he was taken ill.

What would it be like to go again to this place after several owners had lived in it and changed it to their liking? What would the well loved plants look like after thirty years?

It proved a disorienting experience.

Frost had called his five acres *Pencil Pines* because he said he had never made a penny from anything that did not involve the use of a pencil. The South Florida acres acquired by the illustrious American poet held straight-up Dade County pine trees, which gave the name the double twist so frequent in his poems.

On this visit, however, we were able to locate only one lonesome pine.

The cottages were a similar story. All the familiar plants surrounding them, once so scrupulously tended, were gone, swept away by time and expansion. Nobody who ever visited the twin cottages with the picket fence to enclose them would be likely to forget the beautiful white bauhinia. It was one of Frost's favorite flowering trees. Once I helped him transplant some pinkish pentis from our terrace to that spot. Once, when I was clearing out before the arrival of a photographer, he picked up a pail from the doorstep and said: "They oughta' get me kickin' the bucket."

After all these years, a bronze plaque by the front door pronounced the buildings' official status: *Dade County Historic Site*, but there was nothing of Robert Frost, either outside or inside the little houses. There was no possible way to be lonesome for the friend who once lived there because there was not a trace of him any place around.

A new twist was provided to the story of *Pencil Pines* just as we were about to go to press when it developed that the owner was harboring horses, goats and other of God's creatures in the back of the property.

Helen Muir revisiting Pencil Pines.

Our first thought was that we wished some White Wyandotte hens might be introduced into the mini-animal farm. Because it was poultry that attracted Frost to farming in the first place as the twentieth century was dawning. In 1900 he carried baby chicks from Methuen, Massachusetts, to Derry, New Hampshire, where so much of his important poetry was born during the next decade.

When we discovered that there were chickens residing at *Pencil Pines* we wondered if this might not be reason enough to call up the ghost of Robert Frost to pay a return visit to *Pencil Pines*?

The final dramatic twist involved the disclosure that the sale of the entire property excluded the Frost cottages. The owner had confided that she intended picking them up and moving them to another location.

For those of us who knew Frost, away from the limelight of a presidential inauguration and trips around the world, the three decades since his death have been similarly disorienting.

When Kathleen Morrison, who managed Frost's life in every detail after the death of his wife in 1938, broke her vow to herself not to write about the poet and published *Robert Frost: A Pictorial Chronicle* in 1974, she wrote me about the decision.

She was influenced by the shock felt by Frost's friends at what Lawrance Thompson of Princeton had brought forth in the official biographies, particularly the second volume, which earned Larry a Pulitzer but transformed the image of Robert Frost in a sudden sweep as critics picked up the Thompson interpretation of events in Frost's life. *The New York Times* referred to Frost as "a monster" and "a disastrous parent." In a second review, also in the *Times*, the critic declared Frost would not be a person with whom you would care to be "in the same room."

I was peculiarly situated, being around the edges of all the different Robert Frosts, and had not only mingled with Thompson but considered him a friend. I recall thinking it odd when he referred to his first book after Frost's death, *The Selected Letters of Robert Frost*, as "an ice breaker." I reviewed the book, introduced Larry when he spoke to the Friends of the University of Miami Library, and remember one evening at our house when he said in some amazement at a small gathering that "Robert is like another person." I read this, if I thought of it at all, as a flattering remark by a guest.

Letters of protest were printed in the *Times* after the Thompson publication but as late as September 21, 1975, the book editor of *The Miami Herald* used as a lead for his Sunday column this gratuitous slam:

"With the possible exception of Robert Frost, who managed the singular feat of being widely beloved without being in the least bit lovable, Ogden Nash was the most popular poet of his time." This was a distinct change from the year 1915 when Frost was hailed in the Boston press as "the most lovable man in America."

The protest letters in the *Times* from authentic literary figures suggested that Larry Thompson had perhaps learned to dislike his subject and had missed the subtleties of Frost while applying himself to gathering facts.

Thompson died of a stroke in the middle of Volume Three and it was finished by an assistant, R. H. Winnick. Kathleen Morrison dedicated her book to Thompson's memory out of respect for the long years of labor and it is now concluded that the books do provide a wealth of scholarly material. But Larry simply did not have the capacity, humor or delicacy to properly interpret his subject, who it is agreed was complex to a degree.

The "monster" image never did take hold universally, certainly not with most lovers of Frost's poetry.

Mainly, it gave critics a bad name. As Kathleen Morrison said, "only third rate readers believed it."

A few years back I broke my hand and was closeted with a group in therapy for months. One day as I worked on the hand I said, "Miles to go before I sleep."

Down the long table where we all tested our strengths and weaknesses a young Cuban gave me a shy smile. Then he said softly, "Robert Frost."

It happens all the time, whether in automobile advertisements (without benefit of quoting the source), or a feature story on something other than poetry. All Frost wanted, he said over and over, was to have a few poems that would "stick like burrs."

That he did, grandly and positively.

One can be relieved that this sensitive spirit did not have to live through the revisionist period, although toward the end of his life he expressed to me deep concern about his decision to name Thompson his official biographer, a choice Frost had made impetuously immediately after the death of his wife, Elinor.

Relief for those who found the Thompson conclusions painful came in the form of such important books as *Frost: A Literary Life Reconsidered* by William H. Pritchard of Amherst, whose steady appraisal released in the Fall of 1984 restored a clearer picture of Robert Frost, causing *The New York Times* critic Christopher Lehmann-Haupt to lead off his review with this comment:

"First there was the wise New England farmer-moralist, the cracker-barrel sage who became the favorite poet of thousands. Then came the three-volume official biography by Lawrance Thompson—nearly 2,000 pages filled with rage, self-centeredness, jealousy and charlatanism—and the image was transformed into what many regarded as a species of monster in human form."

Pritchard pointed out that Thompson was "uncomfortable with the playful, complicated, devious Frost" and had "little sense of humor; his command of irony was not subtle."

Other books such as *Into My Own: The English Years of Robert Frost* by John Evangelist Walsh (1988) and *Robert Frost Himself* by Stanley Burnshaw (1986), have taken up the cause of restoring a more favorable picture of the fascinating man who continued to break records in popularizing his work as a poet until the end. In my view he was a kind of innocent, certainly of Victorian persuasion and large human contradictions, a man of strong passion and convictions with poetry the driving force in his life, but, in his late years, politics running a close second.

The bulk of his life, the deepest part, was spent with his wife, Elinor, and their children. Much of his important poetry was created during the early years on a farm in Derry, New Hampshire, where the old farmhouse has been meticulously restored by the State of New Hampshire, thanks in some large measure to his late daughter Lesley Ballantine's efforts.

It presents a picture of another time and of a family entirely unique and devoted to poetry.

Each step of the way, through some torturous events, Robert Frost maintained responsibility for members of his family until the end.

His life was family centered and that is the way it stayed.

It seems that the interest in Robert Frost only increases as time goes on and as recently as September 26, 1994, readers of *The New Yorker* were being treated to a lengthy exploration of Frost's poetry by Joseph Brodsky who was asking a question.

"Would you like to meet Mr. Frost? Then read his poems, nothing else." It has the "sound of sense" which is what Frost strove for in his poetry but, at the same time, Brodsky was suggesting that with "a sensibility like this, there is very little hope of real conjugality. . ."

I am suggesting in this account of mine that there *is* such a possibility.

Frequently the question has been asked: How did Robert Frost and I become friends? I always respond the same way: I went to interview him and we liked each other.

It was simple enough, if anything connected with Frost could ever be described that way. I rang the bell of a nondescript little house on Ohio Street in Coconut Grove and Robert Frost answered the door. Moreover, he continued to open doors in a deepening friendship over a period of twenty-two years.

I remember the date because it was my fifth wedding anniversary: January 23, 1941, and I was arriving without warning, you might say, only because there was no telephone in the little rented house. The novelist-poet Hervey Allen had provided me with the address when he told me that Frost had arrived in Miami to attend to building a house.

I found this news titillating. The prospect of the voice of New England being beamed from Miami was off-beat enough to send me straight to Robert Frost's door-step.

After the interview I wrote in my journal: "Robert Frost was charming to me." I didn't know it then, but that was mostly the way it would be until his death just before his eighty-ninth birthday in 1963.

In her letter to me, Kathleen Morrison said of her book: "I left Florida out of it."

In my response I wrote that I'd have to take care of it "one of these days."

That day seems to have come.

1
'WE SHALL STRIKE FOR FLORIDA'

Miami gave Robert Frost a cold reception when he arrived with his wife, Elinor, in December 1934 seeking a place to live for the winter months.

Their doctor in Amherst, Massachusetts, had ordered them south for their health, and Elinor's expectations included finding a house for twenty-five dollars a month. After settling into the downtown McAllister Hotel on the banks of Biscayne Bay for a few days, they saw the unreality of such an expectation. The scarcity of money was a given in their lives, although there was now a vast improvement in accumulating income by means of academic alliances and lectures.

It was one of those lectures that had provided the reason for picking Miami as the way to obey their doctors orders. The poet had accepted an invitation to make the final address at the University of Miami Winter Institute of Literature at which his friend Hervey Allen would speak.

The Frost talk was due in the Spring so the plan was to find a simple cottage in which to live until then.

Winters were always a threat for Robert Frost, now nearing sixty, the fear being that heavy colds would develop into pneumonia. Autumns were threats, too, and demanded flights to Franconia, New Hampshire, because of allergies. For that matter, Frost had spent more time in bed away from school during his childhood than attending classes for the same reasons. His education was largely made up of reading aloud by his mother, the Scottish-born Isabelle Moodie Frost, known as Belle. A teacher, she too had written poetry and never neglected it in the material covered with her two children, Rob and Jeanie Florence.

The poet who wrote of "inner" and "outer" weather and his wife, Elinor, were getting a dose of both in 1934 but the "inner" was harder to bear than the freezing South Florida weather.

Their beloved daughter, Marjorie, had died just seven months earlier of childbed fever—after delivering her first child, a daughter named Elinor Robin, in Billings, Montana. Six children had been born to Elinor and Rob Frost. A childhood illness, a newborn's death and now the loss of Marjorie had left only three: Lesley, Carol, and Irma.

When Marjorie had accepted the proposal of marriage from Willard Fraser, she had written her father: "He is like you, Papa, a Victorian gentleman." And when she died, her mother wrote this to their daughter Lesley: "Papa says her courage and nobility will make death seem simpler and easier when it comes to him."

Before death claimed Marjorie, Frost had written Lesley: "Even in her delirium she is the same old Marj in her talk, grim, ironical and noble. . . . I don't know what will become of Elinor if we lose."

People had commented on Robert Frost's stoicism in the weeks of uncertainty preceding Marjorie's death. The Frosts had hurried to her bedside and arranged for her to be flown to the Mayo Clinic, where, after weeks of intense suffering, she died.

No surprise to find the poet rising to the sorrow. He considered bravery the most important ingredient of being human and drove himself to achieve it.

In November, Elinor was writing daughter Lesley: "It looks now as though Papa really intends going south. I have expected he would back out." A follow-up letter struck a high note: "We shall strike for Florida."

It was the same bold spirit that had taken the Frosts and their four surviving children to England in 1912 where his reputation was unexpectedly made.

Only this time they were not riding into the future. Instead, they were picking up the broken pieces of the past.

The letter to her daughter carried no mention of Elinor's serious heart problems, only that it would be worth the effort "if Rob could avoid pneumonia."

So here they were, in a strange land, in a place calling itself The Magic City and billed as subtropical, only to find the steam heat of the downtown bayfront McAllister Hotel the main comfort against temperatures that dipped as low as twenty-four degrees.

Sitting in the lobby reading the newspapers to attach himself to the new place, Robert Frost learned that no less an authority than the president of the bank was comparing the weather to the "famous freeze of 1895."

The Miami Daily News, the oldest newspaper in the thirty-eight-year-old city, was putting a favorable spin on the calamitous temperature by showing photographs of ice-laden trees.

"Winter's icy breath brings beauty to trees in South Miami," insisted the headlines.

There was nobody to turn to since everybody at the University seemed to have had left town for the holidays.

Frost was acquainted with the British poet, Edward (Ted) Davison, who was teaching that winter at the University, but he had fled for the Christmas break along with the others. Hervey Allen was spending the holidays at his Maryland estate, *Bonfield Manor*.

Elinor had begun to refer to Rob and herself as "befuddled travelers."

Looking around, they wondered what the next step should be?

From their perusal of the newspapers they were gleaning certain facts in attempting to get their bearings. Cuban officials were trying to run down Gerardo Machado, their former president, following his overthrow after the Cuban Revolution of 1933, charging him with "murder and other offenses." So far, he was eluding his pursuers and had just skipped out of Germany.

Hotel entertainers were singing *June in January* and still applauding the death of Prohibition a year earlier—although it had been blithely ignored in Florida while it was in effect. U.S. Senator William E. Borah was preaching to fellow Republicans that "Unless the Party is reborn it will die" and Dr. John F. Condon, Jr., the retired New York educator who had injected himself into the Lindbergh kidnapping case using the code name *Jafsie*, had arrived in Florida "to pursue clues."

There was plenty of news, some applicable to the Sunshine State, none more so than the claims of the Greater Miami Chamber of Commerce that, in the year 1933, it had received a total of 3,269 inquiries from prospective tourists, whereas this year at the same time a total of 4,674, an increase of forty-three percent, had come across its desk.

Attorney General Homer Cummings was warning of "an intolerable breakdown of law and order" as 600 delegates were leaving Washington, D.C., after a national crime conference. The attorney general was pointing out that there had been 1.3 million serious crimes in 1933 and three quarters of them had gone "unpunished."

There was inflammatory talk in the nation's capital of "old age pensions," and in South Florida, there was a meeting on the Miami Biltmore Hotel terrace between United States Congressman J. Mark Wilcox and Julius F. Stone, Jr., to talk privately, concerning FERA, the Federal Emergency Relief Administration, to which Stone had been appointed administrator. It followed an appeal by Key West to the State of Florida for assistance. The city was broke.

In the end it would be FERA that would help the Frosts find a house to rent—but that did not necessarily mean that the poet Frost would approve of its existence.

He was heartily opposed to all the New Deal notions and would declare his opposition many times in and out of poetry.

Social Security was one year away from being enacted.

Considering the various factors involved in their situation in Miami, the Frosts decided to take the train to Key West and see what the island city had to offer.

The poet declared later that the train ride was "the closest thing to walking on water" and the road to Key West led to lodging in the form of the first floor of a house at 707 Seminole Street.

The rental was thirty-five dollars a month, and at first the Frosts were reluctant to settle on it because the owner, a woman, lived upstairs and it was feared the sounds overhead might prove distracting for Rob. Not until it was established that she had no radio and was out of the house a good deal of the time did they sign up.

The search for housing was doubled for them by the fact that quarters were also required for their son, Carol, his wife, Lillian, and the Frost grandson, Prescott.

The connection between Elinor and Rob and their children was intensely close. It began that way on the farm in Derry, where family life was both isolated and rich in attention paid to each member. Rob and Elinor taught their children at home. Poetry and the imagination flourished. They called it "playing school."

On the way to Florida the Frosts had stopped in New York at the Webster Hotel for a Thanksgiving dinner with daughter Irma, her husband, John Cone, and their son, Jacky.

Irma was showing clear signs of the mental instability that had befallen Robert's sister, Jeanie. When Marjorie was so ill, her father wrote to Carol to suggest that he not inform her of the situation until it was absolutely necessary because of the "terribleness" of it.

This Christmas Day in Key West the parents would be without children or grandchildren, an unusual state of affairs at an unusually sad time, but Carol and his family would arrive from Shaftsbury, Vermont, immediately after.

Lesley, the elder of the three remaining Frost offspring, had taken a flight from Chicago to New York and had written a newspaper article about it. This happened over the Christmas vacation from Rockford College where she was lecturing and running a cultural center.

Her father wrote Lesley from Key West exhibiting encouragement and praise about her article: "The writing runs free and the result is a work of one kind of art."

In the middle of writing the letter he got up and went out to measure the distance from house to water, then returned to record that it was exactly seventy-five feet. At the same time he picked up a "grass burr" and enclosed it for his granddaughters, Elinor and Lesley Lee Francis.

Frost signed his letters to his children "Papa" but was known to write "Grampa" when writing his grandchildren.

The Key West house faced a sea wall and beyond it the constantly changing pattern of the water provided a view. But there were problems as well, such as the help from a nearby hotel using "for tanning" what the Frosts had assumed would be their own private beach.

At the time of renting the place Robert Frost was told that John Dos Passos might occupy the upstairs. "My God!" Frost exclaimed. "Two authors in the same house. It would be a regular word factory."

Immediately he fancied it had been indiscreet and described it to Lesley as "an unguarded moment and made enemies of Dos Passos and Ernest Hemingway." He urged his daughter to let the story "die if it will."

It was a typical Frostian weaving of a story, part fantasy and part the family approach to reality.

In another vein Frost wrote his lifelong correspondent, the poetry anthologist Louis Untermeyer:

"Hemingway is said to be here much of the time. But he knows not me and I know not him."

Despite Frost's disapproval of the emergency measures to rescue the flat broke Key West, it was the FERA that came to the rescue again in finding a place for Carol and his family when they arrived. They drove down from Vermont and claimed an apartment close by the Customs House and Post Office for a low price.

All things considered, Robert Frost's view of Key West that winter of 1934-1935 was not precisely admiring. He referred to it as "a hotbed," comparing it to such spots as Greenwich Village, Santa Fe and Montmartre, all in his opinion "arty Bohemias."

The one enjoyment the frail Elinor experienced during their stay was visiting the Old Island Trading Post where Jessie Porter Kirke, whose roots were deep in Key West, made her feel at home. It became a custom for Robert to drop Elinor off there when he went to do the family marketing. Elinor's health had not responded to the change of climate and she thought it was the "dampness."

"Miss Jessie," as the townsfolk generally referred to her, was the granddaughter of Dr. Joseph Y. Porter, the man credited with wiping out yellow fever when he served as the first director of Florida's State Board of Health. Following the death of her husband, she remarried and became Jessie Porter Newton which caused Charles H. Baker, Jr., the dean of American food writers, to give her a new name: "Jessie Porter Rootin' Tootin' Newton."

Miss Jessie did more than her share of beating the drums for Key West and began calling Robert Frost "Marse Robert." Later on, a sign with his name on it would be placed over a cottage on her old place, Heritage House, at the present time run as a tourist attraction relying heavily on the fact that the poet visited Key West and sat in Miss Jessie's garden, resulting in its recent designation as a literary landmark.

In the years following, Frost played tennis with Pauline Hemingway and exchanged humorously barbed conversations with the poet Wallace Stevens.

It would be touch and go for some time as to where Frost would establish a permanent winter home, and as late as 1940 he would be casting an eye out for a place to buy in Key West.

But in the Spring of 1935 Robert Frost had his mind on the talk at the University of Miami to close out the winter series. He learned to put a light touch on these talks, calling them "barding around," but in actuality they put food on the table. These talks had not come to Frost easily.

The first time he had attempted to "say" one of his poems before an audience (he was strict about "saying" and never "reading" them) he was so overcome he had to turn it over to somebody else. He cured that one night by filling his shoes with pebbles. There was blood in his socks when he finished but it served to cure him "by putting his mind on something else," as he put it.

On the way down to Florida there had been four such engagements, each one earning the poet from two hundred to three hundred dollars.

One had been a particular triumph, a talk before the National Association of English Teachers meeting in Washington, D.C. where Vice-President Henry Wallace also appeared on the platform. "I think this will be the hardest thing Papa has ever done as he is the last of three," Elinor wrote. Later, she reported that "the whole crowd rose in homage as he stood up—and clapped with great enthusiasm when he finished."

It was not her habit to attend these talks so it is presumed the report came from the poet himself.

But now, with the first Florida winter ending, the money was beginning to "melt away," Elinor wrote Lesley.

Robert Frost in the Spring of 1935 when he made his first appearance at the University of Miami.

2

THE UNIVERSITY CONNECTION

Robert Frost and Hervey Allen were not unacquainted in the 1930s when the Frost Florida story began. Their first meeting had occurred in 1927 in the second year of the Bread Loaf Writers' Conference in Ripton, Vermont. Connected with Middlebury College, it preceded the University of Miami Winter Institute of Literature.

Poets and other serious writers needed to be heard and such conferences provided that opportunity in addition to the added stimulus of companionship with one's peers.

More than that, it was a recognition on the part of professional writers that they had much to add to the teaching offered by academics who heretofore had been the main instructors in what came to be known as creative writing, a term Robert Frost despised.

One of the first to show an interest in the Bread Loaf operation, Frost wrote to Wilfred Davison, dean and later president of Middlebury, evincing an interest and suggesting that he lead a course in "Responsibilities of Teachers of Composition." The suggestion was not taken up, although Frost appeared on programs off and on.

Frost remained a leader in the thinking that led to Bread Loaf and at one time was mentioned as a potential director but never received the nod.

Both Frost and Hervey Allen played roles in Bread Loaf. Other interesting little similarities present themselves in the way each approached finding his place in literature. Certainly Hervey Allen played a key role in the life of Robert Frost in Florida, where he himself was a leading figure.

In the case of Frost, the story has been told many times of how the virtually unknown poet, as the age of forty loomed and not long after receiving upon his grandfather's death, the farm where he had been eking out a living, sold the farm and, with his wife, boarded the British ship *Parisian*, bound for Glasgow with a cargo of apples and wheat and four excited Frost children.

The date was August 24, 1912.

The children were Lesley, aged thirteen, Irma, nine, Marjorie, seven, and the Frost son, Carol, ten years old. The first born, a son, Elliott, had died at the age of four. A sixth child, Elinor Bettina, had died two days after she was born.

The journey was far more than a sea change. It was a declaration of independence, and for Robert Frost it was a step out of isolation into a world where poets gathered to exchange ideas and hopes and where Rob talked to people who knew what he was saying. He made the best friend of a lifetime, Edward Thomas, a known writer, and persuaded Thomas to turn to poetry.

Edward Thomas was "like the brother I never had," Frost once said. When he was killed in World War I it was a lasting loss.

It has been said many times that Frost took off for England with a calculated plan to court fame and fortune and return to his native land a recognized poet.

It did happen but the way it all happened was far more accidental.

Uncertain as to whether to flee to Vancouver or England, Elinor and Rob flipped a coin. The buffalo nickel came up in favor of Great Britain. Elinor said that she was glad, because she always wanted to "live under thatch." It would become a much quoted phrase.

What Frost had in mind was an uninterrupted period, free of desultory farming and teaching, either at The Pinkerton Academy or the Plymouth Normal School, where he'd done everything from directing Shakespeare to teaching psychology. Now he considered trying his hand at writing a novel.

Hervey Allen, on the other hand, having emerged from WWI with a stiff knee from wounds suffered in the Argonne, had his heart set on poetry alone.

In the case of both men, teaching was a necessity in order to make a living while embracing writing.

In 1919 Hervey took a job at Porter Military Academy in Charleston, South Carolina, for the practical reason that he could wear his uniforms and not have to purchase civilian clothes.

Fate brought Allen together with DuBose Heyward to form the South Carolina Poetry Society, thereby providing the spark resulting in a new lively interest in Southern literature. Together they wrote *Carolina Chansons*, a book of poetry that helped launch the new movement, overdue since the Civil War.

Heyward, of course, wrote *Porgy and Bess* while Hervey went on to teaching posts at Columbia and Vassar before writing the historical novel *Anthony Adverse*, which propelled him into international attention with what turned into a runaway bestseller. Publisher John Farrar had staked him the fourteen thousand dollars to live on while he wrote the book in Bermuda, where he went with his bride, Annette Andrews, a student from his teaching stint at Vassar. With the success of that first lengthy novel he more or less left poetry behind to embark on a series of historical books.

On the other hand, Robert Frost went to England with a Blickenderfer typewriter in his baggage to be used in case he decided to try his hand at writing a novel.

Poems, already written, some few published in magazines, were, of course, in the special satchel where Frost always kept them, just in case changes came to mind.

In the end, Lesley would type up the poems for her father and Frost would carry them to a London publisher named David Nutt, a name he just happened to pick up. First, he had spread them out in a circle on the floor, picking and choosing before coming to the decision.

The publisher's wife, running the business, liked them, and *A Boy's Will*, a title from Longfellow, who was much admired by Frost, made its appearance. Before leaving England another volume, *North of Boston*, was published.

Frost recalled that Mrs. Nutt was "dressed all in black" but there was nothing funereal about that occasion.

When the Frosts arrived in cold Miami in December of 1934 things were looking up financially. They had reestablished ties with Amherst College which had assumed the mortgage for a comfortable residence for them and lectures were becoming a steady source of income.

To make things even brighter, on March 1, 1935, Robert Frost closed the University of Miami Winter Institute of Literature in a blaze of glory, attracting the largest crowd in its four-year history.

The Miami Herald attempted to tell why "Robert Frost, the man, and Robert Frost, the poet, are universally loved." The reporter was clearly devoted to poetry and referred to the Frost wit as "dry and crustily scintillate as the sleeted white of his cherished New Hampshire Hills." He referred to the "unexpected touch of humor" as the best proof of why "Frost has touched the heart of the world."

Frost himself revealed a few secrets of how he went about creating his poems and they were reported in the lengthy review of his performance.

"I wake up to a day of starting sentences in my head—I hear voices sometimes, although I would not dare say that to a psychologist—and I know that I want to put those thoughts into form." His mother Belle Moodie Frost had also "heard voices" and had published several poems in a California newspaper.

Fascinating was his statement that a poet must live a long time and work forty or fifty years before he "arrives" because he needs that time to "let things happen to him and let things occur."

The title Frost gave his talk was *Before the Beginning and After the End of a Poem.*

He would carry the same talk to Harvard for delivery.

The praise heaped on his head in Miami sent Frost on his way to Foxcroft, Virginia, followed by appearances at teachers colleges in Trenton and Glassboro, New Jersey, before proceeding to Amherst and home. He would be speaking there and at the University of New Hampshire, Dartmouth, Harvard and Yale but none would be any more satisfying than the night at the University of Miami.

Being Frost, he did have to confess later that the University of Miami was on the "wretched" side, but it was more sympathy for its president, the heroic Dr. Bowman Ashe, who labored in the face of monumental financial needs.

Interestingly enough, it turned out that somebody at the university that March night had seen fit to take Frost's remarks down in shorthand. They remained tucked away in the archives until two years after Frost died when the Friends of the University of Miami Library produced them in its December 1965 journal *The Carrell*, offering the words straight from the poet's mouth, so to speak.

Coming straight from Key West to Coral Gables, Frost opened his remarks with comments about the poet Wallace Stevens. Without naming him, Frost reported that "he had three drinks and then brought out what underlay his mind about me. He was afraid that I had written too much." It was typical Frost mockery.

Back in Amherst the question of whether or not to accept the invitation to participate in the summer Rocky Mountain Writer's Conference, where Ted Davison was director, came up.

Elinor was pressing for it because they could travel easily from Boulder, Colorado, to Billings to visit Marjorie's baby, Robin.

Robert was trying to dissuade her on the grounds it was too soon to subject herself to such a journey filled with sad echoes. In the end she won out and they went West.

Before that happened Frost delivered three lectures as poet-in-residence at Amherst. The final talk at Amherst was before the graduating class at the opening of commencement week. Frost called it *Our Darkest Concern* and the political strains were clearly visible.

"Men have always dreamed of Utopia. I suppose Utopia will get us yet . . . Our lives are an attempt to find out where we are standing; in politics we are now shifting between the extreme left and the extreme right.

Twenty years from now I shall expect to find education still leaning a bit to the left—but still human."

A rousing reception in Colorado provided another victory. Frost, still leaning to the right, left with these words ringing in the ears of his audience: "A poet may be concerned with the jails, the poor houses, the slums, the insane asylums and wars; or because he sees no possibility of change, he may try to find what happiness he can for himself and be cruelly happy."

Elinor spent a week with her baby granddaughter while he made the talks.

Frost proved himself a master of diplomacy, achieving not one Harvard bid but three—he was also invited to deliver an ode at the Harvard Tercentenary Celebration the following Fall and in addition serve as the Phi Beta Kappa poet during the same period.

He seemed dedicated to issuing only benign statements to the press during the period, but on the way back from Florida to Amherst, in an interview with a *Baltimore Sun* reporter, he made it clear that he was ready to dip into politics, although he offered a kind word for President Roosevelt.

"I'm not horribly anti-Roosevelt. Henry Mencken bears down on the President pretty hard. . . " He polished off the interview by explaining: "Two lines from one of my earlier verses really sum up my whole viewpoint: I never dared be radical when young / For fear it would make me conservative when old."

Frost was learning to shape the press and had in mind his next book which he was calling *A Further Range*.

Both *The Baltimore Sun* and the *New York Times* printed editorials. The day after the reporter's story the *Sun* reminded its readers that the poet Shelley had declared that "poets are the unacknowledged legislators of the world." Next day the *New York Times* headed its editorial with *Poet in Politics*.

Frost wrote to his friend Louis Untermeyer: "Ain't I wily?"

Yes, he was.

A Further Range captured his third Pulitzer in 1937. He dedicated it, as he did all his books, to Elinor.

In December 1935, the Frosts were back in Florida and renting a house at 3670 Avocado Avenue in Coconut Grove, again under doctor's orders to avoid winter weather and committed to the Winter Institute of Literature.

That winter Frost was saying his poems and making his customary wry comments for a series that included Hervey Allen, Bernard DeVoto, Padraic and Mary Colum and Dhan Gopal Mukerji. It would be his last appearance until March 13, 1944 and would be an important one.

Institute associations were often of consequence. This one marked the beginning of an instant close friendship between Frost and Bernard DeVoto, the critic-editor, and a later falling out which became part of the often stormy relations of these writers and scholars. The Frost-DeVoto association was like an instant love affair that erupted in final disillusionment on the part of DeVoto.

At the time, however, Frost wrote to Benny DeVoto: "You and I without collusion have arrived at so nearly the same conclusions about life and America . . . . I can't get over my not having realized you were on earth."

For his part DeVoto declared in a letter to his agent, Kate Sterne, that the best thing happening to him in Florida was that he "spent at least five hours a day with the greatest living American . . . He is the quintessence of everything I respect and even love in the American heritage."

This happening of discovering each other in Coconut Grove that January turned advantageous to a degree for Frost when DeVoto discovered that Frost would be giving the Charles Eliot Norton lectures at Harvard that March and offered to assist him in any and every way possible.

He proved it by getting Elinor and Robert a house at 56 Fayerweather Street and more important, asking his own close friends, Kathleen and Theodore Morrison, to open their home at 8 Mason Street for a reception for them after all of the lectures since the DeVoto home was in Lincoln and a distance away.

This would amount to a startling and dramatic event in the lives of Robert Frost and the Morrisons as well as DeVoto.

Ted Morrison was a Harvard professor and the popular director of Bread Loaf from 1932 to 1955 who made important contributions to its development during his reign. The Writers Conference ran from 1926 to 1992.

His book of poetry *Notes of Death and Life* had been published in 1935 with a preface by Hervey Allen suggesting that Morrison "bids fair to carry forward in the Twentieth Century the kind of sensitive, thinking comment upon life in poetry that the late Edward Arlington Robinson left off. . . "

The dedication poem, *To Kathleen*, was for his wife and promised to "write no word except with thought of you."

Kathleen Morrison would play a lead role in the life of Robert Frost as the last quarter of his life unfolded. Sadly, Benny DeVoto would accuse Frost of coming between him and the Morrisons and, worse, between the Morrisons themselves.

The words uttered at Bread Loaf in the months following the 1938 death of Robert Frost's wife, Elinor, would be much repeated in literary circles. DeVoto told Frost that he was "a good poet—but a bad man."

3

'I GO FORTH COMPANIONLESS'

The next winter, following the family custom, Elinor and Rob allowed their children to set the course and found themselves in San Antonio, Texas. Because Lesley had elected to take her children to Mexico, they decided that Texas was as near a spot as any for them to gather at Christmas time. So it was the winter of 1937-38 before they found themselves once again in Florida, this time in Gainesville, where Robert would lecture and where they considered purchasing a home. It would be less demanding than Miami, they had decided.

Elinor had undergone breast surgery after cancer was detected, one more concern about her failing health. The hope was that they would settle down in Gainesville for a quiet peaceful winter interlude in a permanent winter residence with their children around them.

That December of 1937 proved everything for which the Frosts had hoped, with a family Christmas at Lillian and Carol's rented house, complete with tree and all the trimmings and surrounded by all their grandchildren including Robin.

In order not to tire Elinor by keeping house, she and Rob had spent an interval in the Brown Cottage at the

Thomas Hotel before renting. But, finally they located a two-apartment place at 743 Bay Street North.

They took over the second floor while Lesley and her two daughters occupied the floor below.

Christmas Day had been idyllic and Elinor pointed out in a letter to her friend Nina Thornton that "the children played all day without quarreling."

Earlier, there had been heated discussion on Lesley's part about the fact that her mother was insisting on taking the second floor. Lesley was pointing out that climbing stairs was not doctor-recommended. Elinor remained adamant, insisting that the sounds overhead would be disturbing to Rob.

Frost was enjoying the Gainesville stay, driving with Lesley over to Stetson University in February to speak, telling the capacity audience "not to attach to his poems undue political and philosophical importance" and to listen carefully, as the poet "plays to your ear." He was suggesting "a willing obedience to the poet's mood and thought until he is finished."

At least that is what the *Stetson Reporter* was saying.

What was pleasurable to Frost were the words written after his talk as a requirement in an examination when a student (his name was Frederich Stich) wrote this about Frost's poems: "They have philosophy but it is a philosophy I can understand."

It was "the sound of sense" for all the world. Frost always declared that college students remained his "best audiences."

In the advance press for the Stetson event, Jessie B. Rittenhouse, a prominent patron of modern American poetry, was being quoted from the 1926 Braithwaite's Anthology of Magazine Verse, in which she spoke of Frost's "great charm," calling him "the greatest American poet of today."

Jessie was updating her material in 1938 and wrote to Frost to inquire about details concerning his being published abroad before his work appeared to any extent in his own country.

On February 27, Frost sat down to respond and wrote explicit details, an unusual concession for him. With the biographical information she had sent spread out before him, he made corrections, informing her that he and Elinor took their family to England because of the "cheapness of peasant life over there and the distance it would put between us and our worried relatives. . . . We didn't even think of publishing a book. We went there to be poor in peace and to live a few years for nothing but my writing."

This letter told of meeting members of a group known as the Georgian poets over there only after *A Boy's Will* was published. He made the point that he had remained an American poet, wedded to his native land, by carefully enumerating the time of meeting with various British poets.

In closing the letter, Frost inquired as to the winter weather in Carmel, California, where Jessie Rittenhouse was residing, and offered the fact that "we tried San Antonio last year but found it dark and chill. We have liked Gainesville, Florida, better. . ."

He didn't mention that they were seriously hunting for a house to buy for the rest of their winter visits to Florida, but enthusiasm for the idea was building within the family.

Elinor and Rob made a careful search to find the house most suitable and made up their minds on March 18 after driving around with Carol to make certain their choice was right.

They decided it was and returned to the house at 743 North Bay Street at peace with their decision.

Elinor preceded her husband and halfway up the stairs she was struck by a heart attack. There was no terrible alarm but Dr. John Henry Thomas was called at once.

When he arrived he declared the situation so alarming that he dared not move the patient. For the next two days the house was under seige while seven attacks struck Elinor Miriam White Frost.

Shut out by the doctor struggling to care for his patient, Frost kept a vigil outside the bedroom door, occasionally hearing his wife's muffled words as she responded to the physician. When he was finally permitted into the room she had slipped into unconsciousness.

On March 20, two days after the first heart attack, his wife of forty-three years was dead "of an acute coronary occlusion." Robert Frost never had a chance to say goodbye, never received a word or gesture of comfort to which he might cling.

Afterwards, a distraught Lesley accused her father of having hastened her mother's death by permitting her to live in the upper portion of the house and obliging her to climb the stairs.

In her grief Lesley burst out at her father, telling him he never should have married and certainly never should have fathered six children.

Lesley told her father that he could not live with her and ruin her children's lives as he had Irma's and Carol's. The man who wrote "Home is where when you have to go there they have to take you in" was finding out that those words did not apply to him.

Robert Frost was in a state of collapse when Lesley and his friend, English professor Clifford Lyons, took Elinor's body to Jacksonville for cremation.

Because of Frost's poor health a memorial service would have to be postponed until the following month. The doctor was warning of pneumonia if his second patient failed to follow directions.

Frost prepared a letter which he sealed with instructions that it be burned with Elinor's body.

Theirs had been a love story ever since high school days, when they shared Valedictory honors and when Frost began his relentless courtship.

Before their official marriage (before a Swedenborgian minister from Rob's mother's church because neither Elinor nor Rob had any church affiliation) they had shared a secret ceremony and had exchanged rings.

Nothing conventional about either of them ever and now it was all over.

Once she had given him back the ring from their private ceremony. In return he hurled his ring into the fire.

But she had rescued it and turned it back to him.

Her father had been unenthusiastic about the marriage, preferring that Elinor continue her college education, although the pair was accepted into the White family after the ceremony.

As soon as he learned of Elinor's death, Hervey Allen arranged to drive to Gainesville to offer assistance to his friend. First, he consulted with the University of Florida authorities, who painted a picture of family disarray.

Carol had packed up and with his wife, Lillian, and son, Prescott, started driving back to his South Shaftsbury farm, the place his parents had given him for a wedding present. He was bereft at his mother's death, had always considered her his main support as he searched for his own identity. He farmed with some success but his poetry had not measured up to that of his father's and, despite attempts to branch out on his own, he had not succeeded and was still virtually being supported by his parents. He had taken to spelling his name with two R's and two L's: Carroll.

Daughter Irma did not come at all to Gainesville. Beset as she was with mental problems, it was probably just as well.

The only comforter on the horizon was Hervey Allen who arrived in Gainesville on March 24 and checked into the White House Hotel.

Hervey Allen and his wife, Annette, in March 1938.

Hervey's son, Richard F. Allen, a writer and professor at the University of California at Berkeley, became privy to a letter Hervey wrote to his publisher, John Farrar, about the experience.

Richard describes it as "scrawls in pencil over eleven pages" and explains: "Father's writing, spidery and eccentric at best, is here, from haste and exhaustion, barely readable. I did not read it until 1979, when Margaret Farrar, John Farrar's widow, gave it to me."

Richard calls it "a feverish and exhausted sketch," outlining the "intense night listening to Robert reviewing his life and going back and forth over whether to hang on himself—evidently he decided somewhere within himself to do so and came out of the crisis."

"I haven't any such experience since sitting up in one of the base hospitals in some of the cold hours of the morning in the war, trying to keep the fellow on the next cot there," Hervey Allen wrote. "You can tell when they decide to let go—or when the decision is made for them. I thought Robert would just elect to go after his wife. He would have. It would have been easy—too easy. He isn't an easy spirit."

Richard added that his father characterized the experience as "a boiled-to-the-bone recital of about six hours wrestling with angels which you weren't even able to admit were there, and had to be casual about, while one of the most complicated and sensitive men of our time lay kind of bleeding to death mentally—and I trying to persuade him it would be worthwhile to stop the wound."

With Hervey Allen that night, Frost relived his marriage and family life, blaming himself. It was a scenario that would be played and re-played over and over in the next quarter of a century with those close to him while honors piled up and the whole world became his stage. "There I went draggin' them along behind me" is the way he usually put it.

Frost chose to quote Tennyson in a poetic thank you to Hervey.

"And I the last go forth companionless / And the days darken round me. /" Frost added: "'But it is written also by the same hand, / Let darkness keep her raven gloss. / '"

He added, "I shall never forget your coming to me with such sympathy, Ever yours, Robert."

Hervey would be entering Frost's life in other important ways.

The day Elinor died, Frost wired Louis Untermeyer, who was lecturing in North Carolina, but had visited the Frosts prior to Elinor's death. Untermeyer canceled several lectures and joined Robert in Gainesville. It would be a month before Robert was ready to return to Amherst for Elinor's memorial service.

Gathering his strength, in mid-April before leaving Gainesville, Robert Frost wrote a poem called *Carpe Diem* which he included in *A Witness Tree* four years later. It held these lines: "The present is too much on the senses / Too crowding, / Too confusing, / Too present to imagine."

Within a month's time he was writing Untermeyer: "I don't know myself and won't for a long time, if I ever do. I am so quickened by what has happened that I can't touch my mind with a memory of any kind. I can't touch my skin any where with my finger but it hurts like a sad inspiration."

Also before leaving Gainesville, Frost wrote his son outlining his thoughts on the approaching memorial service. They included a reading by a friend of some poems Elinor liked and "some not too religious verses from the Bible." Elinor had been staunchly opposed to organized religion. The service would be held in Johnson Chapel at Amherst College where Robert had spoken frequently, and a place he found "beautiful."

He took the opportunity to tell his son, "There was nothing Elinor wanted more than to have you take satisfaction out of that home and farm. I wish you would remember it every day of your life." He signed it "Affectionately, Papa."

Untermeyer helped Frost address cards for the memorial service. Nineteen men were invited to serve as pallbearers. Besides Untermeyer, and much to his surprise, the list included Lawrance Thompson. He would be more surprised in a short time when Frost designated him his official biographer. Another invited pallbearer was Theodore Morrison.

That last connection was also due to strengthen as both Ted and his wife, Kathleen or K. as she signed herself in letters to friends, entered Robert Frost's life increasingly, to the point where she took on duties as Frost's secretary and manager of all aspects of his comings and goings for the remainder of his life.

After the service Robert and his children discussed the disposition of Elinor's ashes. They all agreed she had voiced the desire to have them placed on the Derry farm in New Hampshire. It was there during a half dozen years, Frost often said, that the bulk of his best work had taken place. Robert told his children that he wished to revisit the site alone in order to clear the path with the present owners. After that, they would all meet together at their old home for a family ceremony.

But when he travelled there, he found that Elinor's professed wish to have her ashes spilled along the edge of Hyla Brook seemed foreign now. The changes the years had wrought in the setting made it impossible to visualize it as a final resting place under any conditions, despite the echoes of the living that had taken place there.

When he approached the owner to ask permission to return with his children, bringing the urn containing Elinor's ashes, the woman who answered the door seemed suspicious. She neither knew nor had heard of Frost and said she would have to talk to her husband first. Frost asked permission to walk around and it was granted. Now he realized he was saying goodbye to the most important place he had ever lived.

He carried the urn to Carol's farm and placed it in a cupboard until further thought would supply the appropriate resting spot. In the end both Rob and Elinor's ashes would lie side by side in the Old Bennington Vermont Cemetery. Not surprisingly, his marker reads: "He had a lover's quarrel with the world."

That day was decades away and the problem in 1938 was figuring out a new way of living. Rob Frost had lost not just his companion but his protector and "the unspoken half of everything I ever wrote," as he put it. He referred to her in his poetry "as far as she would permit."

It was as though they made a pact with poetry and with each other. Robert's first poem, *La Noche Triste*, appeared when he was sixteen in the *Lawrence High School Bulletin,* and when he was twenty he had *Twilight* privately published. It consisted of two copies, one of which he carried to Elinor, unexpectedly arriving at St. Lawrence College where she was studying. When he was turned away by Elinor—was it rules or time or individual preference? Who knows?—he took off for Virginia and the Dismal Swamp, as his later poetry attests. But they did marry and shared a lifetime of joys and sorrows—the birth of their first child Elliott, his death at age four of cholera infantum (if only the doctor had been called earlier, could their firstborn have been saved?),—always the nagging worry.

Faced with dismantling the Amherst house, Frost immediately put it up for sale. Following that, he went on to dismantle all the organized parts of his life. He resigned from Amherst College, which agreed to purchase his house. He attempted living with Carol and Lillian but after spending days and nights of tramping around in the woods and even considering building an addition to their house, he decided against that. It was a situation too fraught with emotional undertones.

Frost's next move was to plunge into a heavy schedule of lectures as though to exhibit his determination to go on living.

It all blew up in a sense that summer at Bread Loaf when his bizarre behavior caused not just raised eyebrows but alarms. He drank liquor, an entirely new development, and mixed all kinds of drinks with abandon. Oddly, it seemed not to affect him, but one night, while Archibald MacLeish was conducting a reading of his own poetry, Frost started a blaze in a waste basket as he sat in the audience close to the back of the room, an incident many times recorded by the literati.

That was the beginning of the falling out between Benny DeVoto and Robert Frost, but things began to straighten out for the bereaved poet as Kathleen Morrison arranged for him to take a Boston apartment at 88 Mt. Vernon Street and became a guide for all his future activities.

There was no trip south planned as the year 1940 began. Instead, Frost was laid low by a series of ailments which put him in Massachusetts General Hospital for surgery.

True to form, he sent out joking bulletins. His expressed belief was that "all humor should spring from serious matters and that serious business should be touched with humor."

It was February 1 when he was able to set out for a period of recuperation in Key West, accompanied by K. Morrison and her son, Bobby. The trio spent two weeks at the Casa Marina Hotel and after that, Lawrance Thompson, as the newly appointed official biographer, was put into service and arrived to keep Robert company.

The first evening, as Larry was in his room unpacking, a young man approached Robert seated downstairs before an open fire and inquired: "You're Robert Frost, aren't you?"

As always, Robert was pleased to be noticed and particularly after the young man, Hyde Cox, declared he had been present for the smashing 1936 Norton lectures at Harvard. They struck up a friendship that continued to develop as Frost continued to reach out to make new friends and a new life.

That winter in Key West Frost was looking seriously for a house to buy. K. had advised Larry to notify her if he appeared about to enter into any real estate deal. But he found nothing that pleased him despite long walks looking around.

That was the situation when Hervey Allen appeared unexpectedly with Henry Seidel Canby. The suggestion was made that Frost and Thompson drive up to Allen's Miami place, *The Glades,* with them and enjoy a visit there.

It proved to be a turning point.

4

RESETTLEMENT PLANS

Frost had visited *The Glades*, Hervey Allen's Coconut Grove compound, in what would later become South Miami, many times during the winter of 1935 when he and Elinor had rented the Coconut Grove cottage on Avocado Avenue. He had returned for a visit on one occasion after her death in the company of both K. and Ted Morrison.

It was a familiar place and visiting Hervey, Frost walked around the neighborhood, liking what he saw, and came to the conclusion that this was exactly where he wanted to build his winter home.

He would follow Hervey's example and erect prefabricated houses where he could plant things and walk about on his own land.

Robert Frost, the man whose very name summoned up the landscape of New England was poised to become a Florida landowner.

Being Frost, he had a quip to add:

"If the whole region becomes an airport I suppose we can hope to sell out at a profit short of profiteering," he told Hervey.

Robert Frost was bent on re-structuring his life. A year earlier he had purchased the Homer Noble Farm in Ripton, Vermont, and moved into a cabin on the place, offering the main house to K. and Ted. It was understood that he would take dinners with them, and that this would involve mutual friends, particularly during the Bread Loaf sessions. That took care of summers.

For Spring and Fall, there would be a house in Cambridge, at 35 Brewster Street, that K. would find for him in 1941. The South Florida setting chosen by Hervey would provide the neighborhood environment Frost favored.

Frost wrote to Hervey "all I need is a very few friends to set their hearts right on me . . ." and again ". . . your neighborhood would give me pleasure."

Best of all, Frost had already decided to ask his son, Carol, to take charge of supervising the construction of the new Florida home. Carol remained much on his mind as he picked up the threads of a new life.

Eager to consummate the transaction, Robert Frost sent a telegram to Hervey Allen in midsummer asking if it "wouldn't be a good idea for me to try George Merrick myself" in order to expedite matters. Merrick, of course, was the poetry-writing creator of Coral Gables, but the Frost land sale was in the hands of Martha P. Magruder, a well-established figure in real estate in Coconut Grove.

Meanwhile, Hervey was writing to Mrs. Magruder in mid-July from Maryland to explain that he had put down the one hundred and fifty dollar check at Frost's request, but felt that was "all I can or really ought to do in connection with the purchase of someone else's property." Hervey explained that he was "driving night and day on a book."

Things began to straighten out, and by September 26, 1940, Frost was agreeing to accept title to the land Hervey selected despite a slight flaw in the deed detected by the law firm of Hudson and Cason, which also advised that it was not much to worry about.

A month later the original deed from J. Joseph Williams and Mary M. Williams, his wife, was duly recorded in Deed Book 2099, page 471 of the Public Records of Dade County, Florida. Five acres for the sum of fifteen hundred dollars.

K. had explained in a letter to Mrs. Magruder that "Either Mr. Frost or his son will come down to talk about practical things soon after the last hurricane blows past. He will want to discover about sewage and water."

On October 26, 1940, Martha Magruder sat down to send the warranty deed to K. as requested to put with Frost's important papers.

After taking care of the business details she wrote: "I was so shocked to hear of the great tragedy in the family and hope it will not prove too heavy a strain on Mr. Frost. . . ."

On that same day Frost was writing to Untermeyer: "I took the wrong way with him. I tried many ways and every single one of them was wrong. Something in me is still asking for the chance to try one more. . . ."

Carol had killed himself.

After long hours spent with his father, who was attempting to assure him that he was both loved and useful in the world, Carol had pulled the trigger of the deer hunting rifle and died on the kitchen floor of the South Shaftsbury farm where his son, Prescott, awakened by the shot, found him.

First the unhappy Carol, confused by life, burned all the poems he had ever written.

His wife, Lillian, was in the Pittsfield, Massachusetts, hospital for surgery. Before entering she had written Frost, asking him to pay a visit during the days of October first through the third. He did and talked at length with his son, even asking Carol to promise that he would not take his own life as he had been threatening. Together, they visited Lillian in the hospital and had a pleasant dinner in a hotel afterward. In a few days, Frost returned to his Boston apartment. He had scarcely arrived when his sixteen-year-old grandson telephoned the news. Robert called K. and they arranged to meet at the train station to make the return trip.

Frost would go on for years sorting out his son's life, his weaknesses and strengths, still seeking answers for what he as a father had failed to do. In discussing the details with a friend he would usually say, "To hell with it," to put an end to the conversation. It amounted to an anguished prayer.

The immediate necessity was to make funeral arrangements. With Lillian's endorsement, it was decided that Carol's ashes would be placed in the same plot with his mother's. Later, the poet's ashes, as well as other members of the family, would rest there.

Even the funeral was tinged with an edge of bitterness. When the family arrived, after making specific arrangements with the Old Bennington Church clergyman, they found him talking with someone on the grounds. They waited and waited for him to come to officiate at the service. After thirty minutes Robert declared they would do it themselves.

And they did.

Robert wrote letters to his grandson and daughter in-law, assuring them that he would carry them financially, not to worry, and, in the case of Prescott, expressing admiration for the way the boy had performed, doing all the right things: calling the police first, next his grandfather and even arranging to go and stay with friends until his mother was able to return from the hospital.

Frost set out to fulfill his obligations for lectures. Now, without the Amherst College income, it behooved him to step up the lectures. He also notified his publisher that he would be ready with two books, one a prose work to mark the seventy-fifth anniversary of his publisher, Henry Holt. Robert Frost still had "promises to keep."

As for the Miami house project, he was determined that plans would go forward.

On Oct.ober 31, K. wrote Mrs. Magruder: "Mr. Frost is in Iowa for the week but has sent word that there are several things to plan with you. Because of the death of his son and the illness of his daughter-in-law he must plan differently. He must economize and he must be ready by Christmas with something to live in. He has decided to follow Hervey Allen and put up some Hodgson units.

"Do you know of a good simple carpenter who would, with the help of an unskilled man, bolt the houses together? Also a good mason who could lay the cement foundations? Mr. Frost may come down early to oversee the planting of the houses. . . Mr. Frost is getting nervous and would like to get underway."

Martha Magruder selected Ralph Baldwin Lamb, a respected carpenter who had brought his bride from New York state to Coconut Grove in the 1920s and had lived through the Big Blow of '26. He knew how to build houses to withstand time and hurricanes.

Now Frost was writing to him about assembling the two Hodgson cottages in explicit detail:

"The foundation plan for the rest of the house at the north end will be fifty-two feet long and twelve feet wide, extending two feet at each end and beyond the walls (outside) of the houses already built."

In the two-page letter Frost included details on plumbing, painting and general finishing for the houses.

Frost was writing Lamb from his new Cambridge home where he was settling in.

Martha Coolidge, who grew up in the section commonly known as Brewster Village, recalled for me the curiosity of the children of the community, who constantly called on the new elderly neighbor. He was, Mrs.

Coolidge says, unfailingly welcoming, often providing milk and cookies.

On the other hand, she remembers his annoyance when, grown and associated with the Smithsonian Institute, she was forced to leave a dinner party before he had gained a full report of her activities. His new next door lawyer-neighbor on Brewster Street, Erastus Hewitt, proved a stalwart friend, maintaining a key to the place in Frost's absence.

Moving into his new quarters in South Miami would also provide a built-in environment quite to his taste as he continued to reach out and find a genuine spot for himself, apart from public life.

5

'A Florida Farmer'

Even before the deed was signed, Robert Frost was telling his friend Hervey Allen that from now on he would call himself "a cross between a Florida farmer and a Vermont farmer" while Hervey was a "Maryland-Florida farmer."

In point of fact, Hervey did no farming at *The Glades*, confining all that to *Bonfield Manor*, but one evening, all dressed for a dinner party, he greeted the first guests at the front door with a hose in his hand.

"I don't know what it is," he said, "but I receive the greatest comfort from holding a hose in my hand and watering a plant."

Frost took it beyond that, and his plans for acquiring trees and shrubs for *Pencil Pines* were formulating in his head.

If you did not gather it from his poetry, you would know by observing his daily life that Frost was most at home with nature. Botanizing and bird watching, studying the stars, and digging in the earth were all part of his inner rhythms. Besides the pencil, he considered the ax and scythe his favorite tools.

47

Robert Frost greets students at a reception following a talk on February 6, 1941, at the College for Women in Tallahassee, today's Florida State University.

His interest in the various sub-tropical plants was not superficial, although his annual stays at *Pencil Pines* amounted to only about two months, usually beginning in January after wandering down the East Coast, stopping to lecture at the University of North Carolina before hitting the Florida colleges. A favorite school was Agnes Scott in Decatur, Georgia, where a spare overcoat was kept in readiness should the weather turn cold and where the welcome was always warm.

The plant life in South Florida intrigued Frost and before long he was deep in talk with Dr. David Fairchild, the world renowned plant explorer.

Fairchild and his wife, Marian, had purchased eight acres of bayfront land in Coconut Grove in 1916 with twenty-five thousand dollars borrowed from her illustrious father, Alexander Graham Bell, who, as everybody knows, invented the telephone. They named their place *The Kampong* and proceeded to turn it into their own private plant introduction center, traveling the world gathering seeds.

Fairchild was a likely authority with whom to consult about plantings for the Frost five acres. But the plants without the people would not have been enough, not nearly enough. Once Frost said: "Men are the important factors to remember. They are the soil that brings forth the fruit."

Calling himself a Florida farmer was a kind of mockery at which Frost was expert, but how fortunate he was to be officiating at fresh planting with such compatible next door neighbors as the Elmer Hjort family.

Hjort had left his faculty post at the University of Pittsburgh and with his wife, Nettie, and their daughters, Nettie Belle and Edith, set out in 1936 for South Florida, seeking a climate change for daughter Edith for reasons of health. They were accompanied by Mrs. Hjort's Welsh-born mother, Edith Caldwell—and settled on the ten pine acres adjoining the property on which Frost would build five years later.

Hjort joined the faculty of the struggling University of Miami teaching chemistry and in off hours set about building a small dwelling for all five members of the family.

There was no electricity. He worked with hand tools for three years while clearing the ten-foot-tall pine trees. No telephone or water from a spigot, but there were foxes and occasional large rattlesnakes present at the scene.

At the University, Hjort was elevated from professor of chemistry eventually to dean of the college and the man who established the South campus.

By the time Frost appeared, Hjort had expanded the housing on his land and his mother-in-law was residing in the original house.

Mail was R.F.D. out of Coconut Grove and the Hjorts, the Allens and now Robert Frost picked it up from oversize boxes at the corner of School House and Davis Roads.

The country atmosphere, the neighborliness and competency were the right ingredients for Frost and in the weeks before K. Morrison appeared each winter, he spent many an evening reading poetry aloud at the Allens and the Hjorts.

Reading aloud was obligatory, part of his whole history with both his mother and wife. Over at the Allens, daughters Marcia and Mary Ann recall that often Frost would read poems in progress, something that would be considered a rare treat in many circles but at the Allen menage it took Father Hervey to explain that "one day they would be glad they listened."

One daughter asked plaintively why Frost "sometimes read the poem twice?" Clearly, they had other evening pursuits in mind than listening to a poem being born.

Still, Mary Ann, after her marriage to the geographer Dr. Melvin Marcus, remembers bicycling her first-born over to Frost's house in a basket to request a favor.

Would he please autograph one of his poems for Andrew, the babe in the bicycle basket? More than that, Mary Ann wanted the poem hand written.

"Which one?"

"Something about history," she told him.

Carefully, the poet wrote out *The Gift Outright*, the poem he would read at the Presidential inauguration of John Fitzgerald Kennedy, a televised scene the nation would share years later in a burst of emotion on a snowy day in Washington, D.C.

Needless to say it remains a treasure in the Mel Marcus family.

Marcia, the first Allen daughter, remembers Frost walking over from his house "in the dusk, down the white coral driveway" and says about the evenings spent listening to him read his poetry: "Daddy told us we would remember it later in life. He was right. Whenever I read a familiar Frost poem I hear it with the accents of his rather flat, matter-of-fact, New England voice."

She adds: "Robert was always a good neighbor for us and our other neighbors, the Hjorts. He was friendly toward the young people, although we did hold him in awe and he never was on an intimate joking basis with us."

One of the memories that caused chagrin for the quartet of girls in that period was that Robert Frost and Hervey Allen beat them in a game of softball.

It is a fact that as a young boy Frost's deepest desire was to become a baseball pitcher of note. Baseball games continued at Ripton with the Bread Loaf crowd and with players of all ages for many years at Homer Noble Farm.

Gradually, *Pencil Pines* was transformed. Inevitably, a rock wall was put in place. Inevitably, newspapers sent photographers to picture the Florida farmer seated on it.

At least on one occasion Frost remonstrated with some irritation, claiming it was a most uncomfortable perch and he was weary of being invited to sit on it.

A more serious complaint was registered and with more passion by Grandmother Caldwell who continued to point out that her son-in-law, Elmer Hjort, had built that wall.

Hjort had certainly played a part in all the building, even assisting the carpenter Ralph Lamb with figuring out the bolts to hold down the pre-fabricated houses that Frost shipped in. Years later, a bunch of loose bolts were found under one of the houses. Obviously those were bolts that nobody could figure out.

Rock walls notwithstanding, there was nothing fake about the fact that Frost played an authentic role as a man of the strange Florida soil.

Dr. Robert Read, retired from his post as a curator in botany for the National Museum of the Smithsonian Institution, now living in Naples, Florida, had some thoughts about the Florida farmer. Just out of Cornell

Frost poses by his Florida wall.

and with a job at Fairchild Tropical Garden (named for the plant explorer and fast becoming among the most important tropical gardens in the world) Read was introduced to Frost as the 1960s began by George W. Rosner, who was in charge of the archives and special collections at the University of Miami's Richter Library.

At the time, Rosner was living in one of the Hjort cottages and was suggesting Read as a candidate for occupying *Pencil Pines* as a caretaker when Frost was off on an increasing schedule of world travel. Toward the end of the poet's life this happened.

Dr. Read says: "Mr. Frost had cut a trail through his woods and the first time he took me on a walk to point out what he had planted, he proved to me that he knew each of the trees he had and loved them. He enjoyed the fruits, the mango and papaya, the avocados and citrus trees, of which he had a number of varieties."

One day, the young botanist told Frost that he had experimented with some of the loquats and produced a fairly creditable wine. Furthermore, he had made "a pumpkin pie type thing" from an antidesma tree on the place.

Frost was charmed.

Read and Rosner and, before them, Marie and Donald Gordon, who also had occupied the cottages when Frost was away, saw to it that annuals were planted in the enclosure between the two houses at the time of his winter arrival. After some years of summer house-sitting, the Gordons were permitted to build a house on the Frost acres. Grandson Prescott married

Frost at Pencil Pines cottage.

Phyllis Gordon, whom he had met at the University of Miami.

Each step of the way, Robert Frost maintained ties with all members of the family until the end. His life had been family centered and that is the way it stayed. *Pencil Pines* was a refuge for a man carrying unlimited pain in his soul. It is where he continued to botanize and move toward people. Everything he did had a unique touch, even the way he fertilized his plants.

When he mulched and fertilized his trees he was careful to move the mulch away from the center of the tree in order to nourish the roots. He called the circles of mulch "fairy rings."

When he wanted to say thank you to George Rosner for driving him to the nursery, Frost had a load of top-soil delivered to the Hjort's front yard.

Once he telephoned me to say he was in need of 6-12 for the garden and I delivered the stick form of the repellent. He accepted it, but pointed out he preferred the liquid. So later I returned with the liquid.

"This is ridiculous," he said. "I'll change my pants and we'll go and buy you a box of chocolates."

I assured him there was no need to do that and he said, "I know that, but I want to anyway."

We drove to South Miami, and he purchased the most expensive box of dark chocolates in the drug store. While he was at it, he bought one for himself.

Edith Hjort was the family daughter who was given the task for several summers of keeping up the cottages when they remained vacant. Later K. Morrison took her to Vermont to look after her children at Ripton.

Bea Moss, a *Miami Herald* reporter, and her husband, Bill, a music teacher, were invited by the Gordons to live in the Frost cottage when they were away in the mid 1950s, and they retain warm memories of the spot, despite the fact that she decided to make chutney when the mangos came in and ended up with a bad allergic reaction to the fruit. It coincided with being pregnant, not a recommended combination.

Nettie Belle, the little girl who grew up to become a silversmith and a painter, studied at the Boston Museum School and set gems collected by the poet, who was drawn to archeology almost as much as to botanizing and astronomy.

Once, Frost showed her a white arrowhead, presented to him in Georgia while lecturing. Instantly he wanted to enhance it by having the imagined date of it engraved on the surface. It required diplomacy to convince him it was not a laudable idea. Nettie Belle says, "We got to know a warm human individual as opposed to the celebrity."

Getting to know Frost was to accept his occasional petulance. Once he threw a head of lettuce on the floor when Mrs. Hjort took him to Stang's market for groceries. It was because a woman had pushed ahead of him in line.

A later incident indicated a mellowing. When a woman thrust herself ahead of him in line at the railroad station, he merely waggled a finger in a reproving gesture.

The woman glared and snapped "You old fool." It was a story he enjoyed telling.

One day, I was scheduled to pick him up and bring him over to our house. When I arrived, all was still but with an air of having been recently deserted. After a few minutes, Frost appeared from the woods where he had gone to recover after a telephone call that humiliated him.

As we drove along to our house, he explained.

He had received a call from the telephone company asking him if he realized he had accumulated a bill of more than forty dollars for long distance?

He was mortified, a throwback to the lean days when money was non-existent. This held so permanently that one of the most disagreeable acts for him to perform was to approach a bank teller.

His spontaneous response that day to the telephone company representative was to ask: "Don't you ever read *International Who's Who?*"

Further humiliated by his own words, he had fled to the woods.

When K. Morrison arrived to join Frost each winter the pattern of living changed and as Nettie Belle reported: "the great and the aspiring were invited to tea."

In 1949 Hervey Allen died suddenly, three days after Christmas.

Ricky and Phil Wylie had friends in a night before and I sat beside Hervey watching them demonstrate their latest accomplishment: dancing the rumba.

Hervey turned to me and said somberly: "I'd sooner see a hundred couples doing the Minuet."

Phil and Ricky Wylie tending orchids outside their South Miami home.

It was so typical. The soldier-poet Hervey Allen was an eighteenth century man. When I started writing this book I had no idea that he would keep walking in and out of it.

Hervey Allen was not precisely cooperative in that dawning age of press agentry and was known to have turned down flat a request to appear for a radio interview by the leading man of the hour in that arena, Lowell Thomas. He did this despite the most persuasive pleadings of his publishers, Farrar and Rinehart.

It is a mark of the man and the time that such a stance would be tolerated in the world of publishing.

When he died, I sat at a family service with the casket present at *The Glades* before Hervey was laid to rest at Arlington Cemetery. I told Frost later, because he was not in Miami when Hervey died, that as I sat there I thought of the night I invited Hervey to speak at the Coconut Grove Library and he did—with his friend Robert Frost sitting in the first row and heckling, to the delight of the audience. That night Hervey was declaring that the flood of historical novels that followed his giant success, *Anthony Adverse,* appeared ready to sell the book by featuring bare-breasted ladies on the dust jacket. Hervey suggested a three-breasted heroine would sell far more books.

I told Frost about Hervey's comment about the minuet the night before he died and he remembered that Hervey had sent him off to Cuba with Paul Engle and his wife, Mary, shortly after Elinor died. It had been an effort to divert Frost and also provide Hervey with some book-writing time. He told Frost, "You will be received."

Frost wondered what might lie in wait for him in the nature of ceremony. It turned out to be only a piece of whimsy. All that happened, Frost explained, was that Engle wrote a poem *Cuban Voyage,* describing him as what Robert called "a fallen eagle." It offended Frost in every sense, particularly desecrating his need for privacy. He had put into poetry straight terms about Frost's loss, and to him it was unforgivable.

While death claimed both Elmer Hjort and Hervey Allen, Robert went on for another decade and a half. Nettie Belle felt that he made attempts to fill the void when her father died.

Soon after his arrival, he would buy prime steaks and invite the Hjort daughters to a cookout, directing them to invite their "current young man." One of them, Dr. John Robinson, claimed Nettie Belle for his bride, having "survived and passed inspection," as she put it.

Richard Allen was thirteen when his father died and three years later, suffering from loneliness, he found himself on probation at Phillips Exeter Academy. His crime was joining a demonstration organized by Paul Tillich's son Rene and disrupting chapel.

He was relegated to quarters when Robert Frost arrived to speak before the Lantern Club, the school's literary society.

Richard sat alone in his room, remembering how as a small child he had sat on Frost's lap in the family automobile listening to "The Erie Canal," being sung to him in "more of a droning chant than a tune." It was a low moment for Richard, deprived of contact with a family friend.

It turned out that in the middle of his talk at the Lantern Club, Robert Frost stopped and looked around, asking where his friend's son Richard Allen was.

Breathless fellow students carried the news to Richard as total embarrassment by all hands resulted. The next morning, before Frost left, a reunion was brought about in the presence of numerous faculty and much smiling all the way around.

Years later, when he received his father's letter to John Farrar, it came to Richard that what Frost was doing that day was repaying an old debt to his friend.

"Perhaps what was being remembered that day was when Father arrived unexpectedly to rescue Robert Frost from his deadly grief," Richard mused.

6

'MY FRIENDS CALL ME ROBERT'

That day in 1941 when my Robert Frost interview appeared in *The Miami Daily News* Frost wrote me a note, and, in a postscript, requested five copies of the article "if it wouldn't be too much trouble."

Apparently it was. I failed to answer the kind note and acknowledged it only in my journal: "That dear Robert Frost wrote that he found my piece in complete good taste."

In my own defense, I would point out that those were chaotic times for all of us. World War II was heralding its share of coming burdens and changes, and by the end of the year, Pearl Harbor would burst on us. Everybody was feeling the war, one way or another. Frost had made only one stipulation when being interviewed: "Let's not talk about the war. . ."

I had actually written the interview for North American Newspaper Alliance. At the time, Frost was not enjoying the stature in the press that he later achieved, and NANA turned down the feature. *The News* picked it up. Since I wasn't keeping hours at the newspaper, sending tear sheets was not that simple or convenient.

My personal story was that I had given up newspapering in anticipation of the arrival of our second daughter in 1939 but had taken on Philip Wylie's role as publicist for the Committee to Defend America by Giving Aid to the Allies as a volunteer job when he was called to New York to assume an editing post at Farrar and Rinehart. I was beginning a radio program, *Women In Defense,* on WQAM, as well.

My husband was writing *The Army Way,* a handbook for soldiers, with Phil Wylie and offering his own services in the armed forces.

Later, after being turned down because of high blood pressure, Bill gave up his law practice to study celestial navigation and ended up as a navigator with Pan American Airway's Africa-Orient Division, wearing the uniform of the Air Transport Command on flights as far as the Russian border.

By the Spring of 1941, I was back writing a seven-day-a-week column for *The Miami Herald* while Frost was off gathering important honors, including another Pulitzer, for *A Witness Tree.* He was the one literary figure to garner four in all.

Were it not for our mutual friend Hervey Allen telling me that Frost was asking why we "never asked him around," one wonders if our friendship would have been formed.

Amusingly enough, Robert went from my interview to one at the *New York Telegram,* and the story by Henry Lee began "The last person who would interview Robert Frost was a lady reporter in Florida.

"'She looked down at my feet,' Mr. Frost said today' . . . and said "Why Mr. Frost, you've got baseball shoes on.'"

"'After she said that,' he explained cheerfully, 'I knew that no matter what I said the shoes would be the story. . .'"

I never saw that story until Edward Connery Lathem brought out his *Interviews With Robert Frost* three years after the poet's death. No opportunity to laugh about it with Frost, but it tells much about his approach to the press and his shifting from one approach to another in order to gain attention and be entertaining.

I view it not as duplicity after writing a note of praise, then using the same situation in what might be construed as offensive. I view it as the method developed by a struggling human being of some genius, making up stories along with his poems. He said that he considered each poem "a performance" and the world well knows he became a magnificent performer, a presence not to be forgotten once listened to on a platform.

There appeared to be so many Robert Frosts, each one valid in a different way. Deeply, there was Frost the Poet, who devoted his life to the craft. The Public Man and the Private Man and the Media Man were different souls, all eager to be heard. The Private Man was as complex as all the others, with his family life and his domestic nature the foundation.

He was complex and insecure in his soul, but his reaching out to people he called friends was genuine. This trait was in evidence during the decades he spent

Robert Frost with Annette and Hervey Allen at the Surf Club on Miami Beach.

in South Florida where what began as an interview ended up as a friendship of substance.

The interesting thing about becoming a friend of Robert Frost's was that he made the overtures.

He told Hervey he would like to see me again so Hervey took us to luncheon in his cabana at the Surf Club, which at the time struck me as an incongruous setting for the New England bard. I was still thinking of Frost in a removed way.

As always, the conversation was rich, and I came away satisfied. Before long, Hervey's wife, Annette, reminded me that Robert was asking why we avoided him.

This time I responded with an invitation to tea as 1942 began. The event stands firmly fixed in memory.

Dr. Abraham Flexner, whose contribution as a guide to men like John D. Rockefeller, J.P. Morgan and Andrew Carnegie in their various philanthropies was historic, was staying at a Miami Beach hotel with his playwright wife, Anne Crawford Flexner. I invited them to join us that afternoon.

Dr. Flexner's accomplishments included the history-making reform of medical education as well as the formation of the Institute for Advanced Study at Princeton. He brought Albert Einstein to the United States.

Robert Frost and Abraham Flexner had a wide range of subjects to explore, including the fact that a Flexner daughter had enjoyed classes with Frost. That day, Frost proved something that never failed to surprise: he could hold up his end on scientific subjects in any society.

One of his life themes, however, was to play up the importance of the arts in an age of science. He held to it determinedly—right into the White House.

The fact that Dr. Flexner functioned at the center of power in a fascinating generation of immensely wealthy figures was not lost on Frost, who was insatiable in his fascination with the seats of power as he went about his travels.

My own recollection of that day is deep and personal. The occasion was flawless, as was the cake the Flexners contributed and the incomparable *Somerville and Ross* books to which Mrs. Flexner was introducing me because we were both of Irish blood.

The Smile and the Tear, with the story of the indomitable Julia Dempsey, grabbed my instant attention, and Frost was delighted with the tale of Julia, who took to her bed for years but found the strength to rise and walk the seven miles to the village in order to collect a legacy of eighty pounds.

That day, Bill was occupied with both law and navigation, so it was just our two little girls, Mary and Melissa, to enjoy the tea party.

Mary, our five-and-a-half-year-old, was busy "passing things," but took the time to take Mr. Frost on a tour of the garden, which included her own portulaca flower bed. A garden tour with our first born became an accepted part of his visits after that.

Frost had a keen appreciation of what being a child involved. Once his daughter Marjorie reported that her Father was "good at making up poetry and bringing up children."

From that day, I carry the picture of our second daughter, Melissa, who took quite a fancy to Frost. She was two and a half years old and elected to stand by his side as he sat in one of our wing chairs, talking or listening, occasionally letting his eyes fall on Melissa with a bemused expression while she continued to gaze up at him. They didn't touch, just surveyed each other.

It is no surprise that the picture of Melissa and Frost should be a sharp memory of that occasion because she was killed instantly by a careless driver two months before her fifth birthday in the summer of 1944. I always felt that her death provided cement for a deepening friendship with Frost.

That day with the Flexners, we talked some about the war and about poetry as well. Frost said he did not feel that World War II would interfere with the flow of poetry.

He was correct, in that what it did for him was increase his readers. That happened the following year when the Council on Books in Wartime purchased fifty thousand copies of *Come In* to distribute overseas to the troops.

"Poetry goes on just like marriages," Frost was telling us that day. At the same time, he was declaring that most young poets were inclined to be too academic.

"As Walt Whitman said, 'They cling to the shore,'" he was observing. "They are afraid to strike out. They are so cautious they equip themselves with planks to hold them up. They gather degrees, B.A.s and Masters and Doctors, all gathered so that if they fail in poetry they have three degrees to swim with. I have sat with their parents, answering questions as to whether or not writing poetry would be 'a safe job. . .'"

That day, too, he was deploring the fact that "as a people we are not thoughtful enough" and pointing out that "first we adore Charles Lindbergh, then we hate him. We need a more middle of the road quality."

At that time, we now know Frost was grappling with the fact that his old friend Louis Untermeyer was wanting him to join forces with the Office of War Information, and Frost was feeling that he could never play the role of propagandist and, therefore, was refusing.

In the series of overtures offered by Frost in the name of friendship, the one I remember with a smile happened

*Florida friends Hervey Allen, left and David Fairchild, right,
visit with Frost at the July 1946 Bread Loaf Writers' Conference in Ripton, Vermont.*

at a dinner party when he leaned across the table and hissed at me: "My friends call me Robert." His sensitive ear had picked up the fact that a woman whom he'd just met was calling him by his first name whereas I was holding to "Mr. Frost."

Then, as Frost was preparing to leave *Pencil Pines* for another year, Hervey gave a small farewell party for him. Among the guests were President Bowman Ashe of the University of Miami and his wife, Marie, and Henry and Paula Chapin (she was the daughter of the poet Henry VanDyke and her husband, Henry, was a writer-poet).

As we were leaving, Robert took me aside and asked "Won't you take the responsibility of looking me up next year when I come?"

I promised I would—and I did.

We grew increasingly at home with each other, and soon the friendship embraced the whole family. Our son, Toby, was born in 1946, so once again the Muirs were a quartet and we would continue seeing Robert, both in Florida and, as time went on, in Vermont.

For a while, Toby referred to Frost as "the man with the silver wheelbarrow." That was because of the protective covering Robert applied to the garden tool to insure a longer life in the South Florida climate.

Robert and Toby made their first real connection the night our four-year-old came to the dinner table where we lingered over coffee.

Impatient for his evening reading, Toby thrust at me a small poetry book open at *The Pasture*, one of Frost's early poems.

Robert, seated on my right, had a clear view of his poem. I said, "That is Mr. Frost's poem."

Toby glared. "It is *not*," he said firmly. "It's *mine*." From then on they were fast friends.

The tattered little book, now shorn of any identifying cover or name of publisher, was purchased in Woolworth's by me when one dime could acquire a treasure. Today, it rests in a brown envelope with these words written on the outside: *My Most Precious Book.*

Each year, Robert would arrive in Miami after following a series of college platform appearances, the final one at the University of Florida, and would telephone his arrival if it happened that we were not informed before the date.

Sometimes he'd call right away and ask "Are you having me for dinner?" and I'd say, "Certainly. When do you want to come?"

Occasionally he'd say: "Tonight. Could we have fish and some of those Swedish cucumbers you fix?"

One night, as I was blowing out the candles after dinner, he looked at me gravely and said, "You had nine things on the table tonight. That took a lot of trouble."

Nobody ever said things the way Frost did.

One day he asked, "What time do you get hungry?" I admitted to liking breakfast, lunch and dinner. He shook his head in disappointment.

He despised breakfast, never bothered with it, occasionally took a raw egg, but "got hungry" around one o'clock.

Soon after, he called and invited me to lunch, explaining he had some cold roast beef, but could I possibly get hold of "some bibb lettuce and some of that good bread?"

Frost has been compared to Plato and Coleridge as a conversationalist. Never having been privileged to enjoy the close-up company of the latter two, I can only say what so many others have known well: Frost was superb as a talker.

It was as though our conversations had no beginning and no end. They picked up after months and months of absence during which the poet Robert Frost went on picking up honor after honor, well beyond what might have been imagined way back in the early years of being ignored.

The foundation of our family friendship, it seemed to me, was born around the fire in the days when Robert first arrived and was staying alone at *Pencil Pines*.

Bill and I were the sort who lit fires even when the French doors had to be opened from time to time to decrease the heat, so, as the Frost story unfolded within our family, the fire acted as a backdrop.

It was before our fireplace that Bill and Robert and I had our best and most important talks. It was not until the very end of his Florida stays that Frost had a fireplace installed for himself. In the early days he had a wood-burning stove and chopped his own wood.

My husband had a fire trick which he called the "Adirondack blower." It started a fire instantly and after that, our eyes were drawn to the flames as confidences unfolded.

Death, religion, belief and, of course, poetry were the main themes. Robert referred to death as "the abyss."

My husband's head was filled with poetry he had memorized. I can hear him, after considerable urging, saying the lines from Ulysses "This is my son, my own Telemechus," while Robert gazed into the fire.

We talked about Carol's suicide, Robert going over and over the details of how he failed to convince him that he was a valuable human being who should not consider taking his life—and of Irma, going mad but "not mad enough to be put away" until the night she was discovered wandering around Boston and had to be institutionalized.

Robert had a vast disdain for psycho-analysis and reported how he confronted the doctor who was on staff and had come to sit by his bedside during a hospital stay.

Robert said he asked, "You a psychiatrist?" and the young doctor admitted he was. Robert described what he said: "Jeez Christ."

But in the case of Irma, he was glad enough to turn for guidance to his friend Dr. Merrill Moore, who in addition to being a psychiatrist was also a poet.

I can hear Robert's voice going on and on, late at night, once wistfully remembering that he "spent more time with his children than most fathers."

He had some stock phrases that rose regularly such as "I went my willful way, draggin' them along" as he looked back over the family history.

My husband had been born on the birthday of the second Frost child, Lesley, but a year later. Bill's father, a distinguished Oregon lawyer, died at a young age when Bill was eleven. Robert's father also died when Robert was eleven. Both had been struck down with the scourge of the period—tuberculosis.

Robert said his father "gave him" TB playing with him on a couch. "There is no doubt that I had it as a young man," he told us. "But I never held it against him. He used to beat me, too. But still I never held it against him. I never hated him." One thing Frost never could understand was why his father was so outraged at his wife's using his hairbrush.

His father "had speculated with his insurance money" so that when he died there was nothing, Frost said. "It would have made all the difference to my mother and me."

Another image from Robert's past as a boy in San Francisco was that he "stole things" with a "partner in crime." His first name was Seth and later he turned into "a working criminal," serving prison sentences. Before leaving San Francisco, following his father's death, Robert Frost, the boy, went about "giving presents to some of the people I stole from. . . ."

It was the kind of act that Frost would do, trying to make amends. He told us all this one night around the fire.

There were different avenues of conversation, and we traveled down any number, during which I discovered that being a friend of Robert's meant being on the receiving end of all manner of instructions—perhaps because he followed his mother into teaching or perhaps because of his genuine desire to reach out to influence others.

In any case, he touched individuals as diverse as his devoted followers at Agnes Scott College to the Nieman Fellows at Harvard who one year declared him to be their "favorite experience." This from working journalists from all over the country who were not novices at coming to judgments. Once I heard Frost speak at a Vermont church in Ripton where small children gave him their rapt attention.

What he attempted to teach me ranged from skipping stones on the banks of Biscayne Bay (accompanied by his Border collie, Gillie, or, later, our son's dog, Guy, both of which would have fared better at stone skipping than I) to cautioning me to "be with caution bold."

Laughably inappropriate for a woman harboring four generations at the moment of instruction was "make your own little days and nights."

Of course, this is the man whose loving wife finally gave in on the time of milking cows.

Her poet husband, who made it clear to the world that he was "one acquainted with the night," also made it clear to the cows that the time of milking would be high noon and midnight.

Robert was able to think his thoughts by prowling at night and sleeping until ten o'clock in the morning.

One of the useful offerings of advice from Frost to me was, "If I don't tell them they won't know." He also said it in a poem: "But the Secret sits in the middle and knows."

I never could adopt that one either, but I put to good use one of my favorites of these various instructions. It was when faced with an impossible fellow creature uttering impossible pronouncements you should purse your lips and say, "That's a thought!" Try it. It soothes and works far better than intellectual argument.

The right word meant everything to Frost. Once he arrived in Miami to find his little house bereft of a dictionary. He literally could not rest until he was able to purchase one himself at his favorite bookstore. When called on to drive him there on his first day to correct this serious lack, I elected to wait outside, thereby giving him the privacy of meeting one of his support groups unimpeded by interfering currents.

I am struck as I go back over those times and refer to my journal that so much of our talk was truthful and trusting and with so much less parrying than was his custom.

By early March 1942, Frost was lecturing at the University of Florida and his friend Dr. Clifford Lyons was introducing him as "Robert Frost of the United States," while the student publication *The Florida Alligator* was reporting on the Frost remarks.

"I expect to see two things when I am 150 years old," the poet was telling them.

"With the diffusion of power, people will become more considerate of each other. Two, people will have learned to retain a calm mind during times of stress."

He was also describing his poetry as "a sort of modest description of America."

Memories of my friend crowd the mind as I look back and remember the day when, returning from a walk to the Bay and on our way to the cottage used as a study by Bill and me, I said something of which Frost strongly disapproved.

I was inclined toward jungle with my gardening and enjoyed permitting the birds to volunteer to their heart's content.

This day I told Robert that I had a new thought: I would pick at least one weed each day and at the same time visualize myself eradicating an unfavorable character trait within myself.

He stopped dead still. "Pull the weed," he said severely. "Leave yourself alone!"

I got the message. Leave something up to God.

Robert Browning said it this way: "My business is not to remake myself but to make the absolute best of what God made."

As our friendship continued so did the directives.

A book I wrote in 1953 was published by Henry Holt and not until Robert invited me out on a boat with Alfred Edwards, by then the head of Holt, and his wife, did I realize that Frost thought that somehow he had engineered that publication.

I told him that he had nothing at all to do with it, that I'd signed the contract with others at the helm. But it was a constant surprise to me to find what a close interest he appeared to have in whatever work I did. I never thought of myself as a writer. I was a reporter in my own view.

I was freelancing for magazines after writing the book when one day a neighbor whose husband had just died leaving her in charge of a real estate firm, came to make me an offer.

It was the beginning of a period when women were entering the real estate market in Miami in droves and she was proposing that I join her firm on the grounds that I "knew a lot of people."

When Frost arrived and learned of this he was shocked.

"Stick with the arts," he commanded.

Once again I was surprised at his impression of what I was up to, but not too long after, I found myself back at newspapering, this time as drama critic of *The Miami News* and writing about the arts in general.

Robert never got over laughing about the fact that the poor woman got in trouble with the law over some transaction or other. He claimed he had saved me from the jailhouse.

We had a game we played called "Who do they think they are?"

Frost refused to write "poet" when describing his occupation because "poet was a praise word."

He had used the word "farmer" when it was necessary to attach a name to what he did and sometimes "teacher," on a form—but never "poet."

When Robert first came to our house, we formed a recognition of our family tastes as they compared to the Frost family.

When he learned that Bill had waked Mary up one midnight and carried her up to the roof to observe the constellations, he approved. He had once waked up Lesley when she was ten to see Halley's Comet.

Then, the little shelf Bill had constructed for me next to my bed held bedtime reading in the form of *The Varieties of Religious Experience*, by William James, and a small volume of Emerson's essays borrowed from my mother.

They were there waiting for me when Melissa was killed and then I learned how important both writers were to Robert Frost.

When he entered Harvard for that brief period of study Robert had his heart set on taking classes with William James and was keenly disappointed when they were not forthcoming. Frost was respectful of both these men's minds and particularly Emerson's.

We were riding along Thirty-Sixth Street after mailing off at the airport post office an edited version of a talk Robert had delivered on Emerson. It had been necessary to put it into written form from a tape recording and had been a much-postponed chore that had plagued him.

Robert asked: "Did you ever notice Emerson never wrote about people? No gossip in him. If he'd had a love of gossip in him he might have been a novelist."

I said I didn't think much of Emerson's poetry.

"Never say that," Robert said softly. "He wrote those wonderful words: 'Fired the shot heard round the world.'"

My interest in these two writers gave us an instant connection. We discussed essays like *Spiritual Laws* and

The Oversoul, along with *Swedenborg; or The Mystic*. Robert's mother had embraced that form of religion after being born a Presbyterian in Scotland, later switching to the Unitarian church and finally becoming a Swedenborg follower. Robert was amused when I told him that in a burst of adolescent rudeness I had said to my mother: "You and your Mr. Emerson—don't you ever have an original idea?"

When you consider all the various people and interests Robert Frost was developing during the two decades we knew each other it comes as a bit of a surprise that on meeting my mother he should remember that story and laugh about it with her.

That was the Frost I knew.

No need to emphasize Frost's appreciation for theatre. In London when they first arrived there, Elinor and Rob had made it a point to take in a play immediately and even in Miami there were a couple of nights out for theatre.

One such event was a trip to see Bea Lillie at the Coconut Grove Playhouse.

We sat in the fifth row center, Bill and Robert, K. Morrison and I, Robert wearing his hand-washed pants, pale-blue jacket and canvas shoes (no socks) and enjoyed the incomparable Lillie exhibiting her particular brand of humor.

That night Marlon Brando was in the audience with his host, George Engle, the oil millionaire who had restored a broken down movie house and transformed it into a legitimate theatre, thereby bringing "Broadway to Coconut Grove."

During the intermission people were flocking to the lobby to catch a glimpse of the actor while we remained in our seats. Finally Julian Langner, brother of Lawrence Langner of the Theatre Guild, recognized Frost and came up to pay his respects.

I was interviewing Miss Lillie in a day or so and told her what Frost had said about the show.

"So pretty," he kept saying about the staging.

Another time, after Mary had returned from studying acting in New York, she was appearing in a play by a Canadian playwright, Patricia Joudrey, called *Teach Me How To Cry*.

It was a haunting play staged at Studio M., a little theatre made famous by the fact that Tennessee Williams had held a world premiere of *Sweet Bird of Youth* there.

Mary was playing the lead in the Joudrey play, and when Robert arrived and found out, he was insistent that he be taken to see it.

They put us in the front row which was certainly not my choice for Mary, although Robert could appreciate the acoustics from close up.

During the intermission I whisked him up to the corner where he said: "This will be a whiskey night, won't it?"—in his customarily unique way of saying everything.

He was anticipating a long night of talk about the play in order to digest it and give the occasion its due.

I made a sudden trip to New York in the Spring of 1956 and on my arrival found out that daughter Mary had arranged tickets to attend a poetry reading by Robert Frost at New York University where he would receive the University's Medal of Honor.

As we walked across Washington Square to Vanderbilt Hall I relished the thought of seeing our friend so soon after he had left Florida.

I had an aisle seat next to journalist William MacKaye and observed the large crowd gathered to hear the poet.

Suddenly, the front doors were flung open and out stepped Robert Frost, all lit up for an encounter, aglow with excitement and wearing evening clothes. He was close enough for me to reach out and touch as he made his dramatic entrance.

That night I discovered that his remarks were repetitions of what we had talked about in Florida where he had been lining up his thoughts.

When it was all over I did something that Robert did not later understand. We left without speaking to him. Why had I not come up to talk with him afterwards?

I never quite realized myself why I had not done so but while writing this book, I asked my daughter if she had any thoughts about it?

Her reply was clear cut.

Mary said: "I know why you didn't. It meant more to have the private Robert. The public part really took him away.

"He came into our house with that low rumbling voice and wanted to know everything about us. He said everything in a different way. He was always seeing the entire world in a fresh way."

7

'LIFE: IT GOES ON'

An interviewer was asking Robert Frost: "What do you think about life?"

It was one of those questions, but this time Frost didn't respond with "That's a thought."

What he did say was: "It goes on."

It certainly was going on for him.

He had set several stages on which to play out the final decades of his life, and the Florida encampment was beginning to be turned into a family compound.

It began when his grandson Prescott, who had enlisted in the Army, received a medical discharge after suffering a case of his grandfather's old complaint—pneumonia.

By the Fall of 1943 Frost was busily rearranging lives and planning for Prescott and his mother Lillian to spend the winter at *Pencil Pines*.

As he set out on the series of talks that supplied them with income, he was making it clear where exactly they would sleep in the two cottages. They would occupy the two rooms of the smaller house while Robert would keep the bedroom in the three-room house for himself.

He used the word "always" in a letter to make no mistake about it. He explained that the sitting room and kitchen could be used for all members of the family.

The biggest change occurred when Frost gave his daughter Lesley 1.55 acres of his land as a wedding present in the summer of 1954. On it, she and her new husband, Joseph W. Ballantine, built a handsome house facing Davis Road.

An expert on Far Eastern Affairs, Ballantine had been teaching at the University of Miami following his retirement from the State Department.

There were similarities between Lesley and her father and resultant tensions under the surface.

Named for the "Bonnie Lesley" of Robert Burns fame, she called her father "Rob" and her siblings "the children" until she was six years old.

She would never accept that her father wrote the poem *The Silken Tent* for K. Morrison and insisted that she recalled first hearing the lines when her mother was still alive and all poems were made with Elinor Frost in mind.

How easy to understand that the little girl who was home-taught from birth by two parents, learning about metaphor and poetry and experiencing that unique family life, should hold that view.

Her writing tablets from childhood and copies of *The Bouquet*, the little magazine she and the other children published in the idyllic days in England, where their days were spent with other poets and their children, were part of her history and deeply embedded in her nature.

But you did not share intimacy with both father and daughter at the same time, perhaps because of the important role K. Morrison played in Robert Frost's life.

Robert took Bill and me with Lesley and K. Morrison one evening to test it out. Seated in the El Dorado dining room, part of an early Coconut Grove rustic enclave for winter visitors of a certain cut—those who craved simplicity and were acceptable to management—I was on Lesley's right with my husband on her left while Robert headed the table with K. on his right.

Father and daughter's eyes were of the same arresting blue and as she expounded on politics and communism her cheeks became very pink.

I felt an enormous sadness that night turning from one handsome head to the other as Lesley, who had been associated with the State Department for some time, described how she encouraged Senator Joseph McCarthy as he entered the chambers for the McCarthy Hearings in Washington by calling out, "Don't let them get you down, Joe."

Her father was muttering, "She's crazy" from the other end of the table but she didn't hear it. Crazy was a word he used with a particular emphasis. It was a word with which he was "well acquainted."

After she built the home, Lesley gave a large reception during a visit from her daughter, Elinor Wilber. It was the night before Robert was due to depart for his various engagements before returning to Vermont. Bill and I were committed to a dinner at Miami Beach, but we went by Lesley's briefly before, and it was an odd sensation to walk down the line and be "received" by Robert.

Later, when we returned from the Beach, I decided to drive over, although it was ten o'clock, and say a proper good-bye to our friend. The winter stays were short enough and while farewells were not among Robert's favorite things, nor mine, I felt the need for a final salute.

Would I be coming up to Ripton? Robert wanted to know. I shook my head.

"You have a lot on your plate," he said—and then "Ya know we want ya." It was reassuring, and of course, what I wanted to hear.

My usual memory of good-byes entailed Robert standing under the rose apple tree in our driveway waiting to enter the car for Bill to drive him home.

One night, Toby got out of bed at two a.m. to give Robert a sendoff by singing "I Heard the Bells on Christmas Day."

He sang it over and over before getting it the way he wanted it. He was not showing off. He was confounded when his voice, froggy with sleep, refused to hit the proper note. Toby went back over it several times before hitting the note perfectly while Robert and Bill stood patiently by the car in the driveway.

Toby was in the St. Stephen's Boy Choir and wanted to get it right. Robert understood that perfectly and thanked him for the performance.

In the summer of 1951, the Muirs had changed the locale by visiting Ripton and at Bread Loaf we learned

Summer of 1951 in Vermont, left to right are Anne and K. Morrison, Robert, Ted Morrison's brother, and Helen. Toby Muir (age five) stands next to RF.

that to get around the question of formality versus informality, most of the habitues of the Writer's Conference referred to Robert Frost as "RF." Even Lesley and other family members were beginning to call Robert "RF."

John Ciardi declared that he knew he was "in" with Frost when he signed a note with the one word "Robert."

It was interesting about how nearly everybody felt about Robert. Even now, writing this book years after

Left to right is John Ciardi, Ted Morrison, RF, K. Morrison at the Bread Loaf Writers' Conference in Ripton, Vermont.

so many are dead and well buried, when I ask those who are still around what they recall about Frost so many of them use the word "presence." From adults who knew him as children to an important newspaper editor like James Bellows, the word comes to their lips.

Bellows, who sat on a couch with Robert for hours talking, used the word.

*K. Morrison and Bill Muir returning to the Homer Noble
Farm barn in the summer of 1951.*

My recollection of Robert's reaction that evening was
that he asked, after Jim and his wife left, why *she* had
paid no attention to him.

Much as he believed in himself as a poet, Frost was
never certain of how he was being received.

About John Ciardi: Robert's remark was entirely
Frostian. He said that "Ciardi kissed every woman in
the room except his wife."

One afternoon, Robert came down from the cabin
and found me stretched out on a blanket soaking up
sun in front of the Homer Noble Farm. He joined me
and we set about our customary free wheeling conversation. I reported on the flavor of Frost's farm helper

Stafford Dragon's dancing, which I had experienced as a partner the evening before at the regular square dance, thinking it would amuse Robert. It followed standard procedure for our conversations in Florida, but that evening when I saw K., she warned me to be careful in talking of such things with Robert. I was being put on alert.

It would amount to a shift in position in what was said and not said, I felt. Later, it did not seem to affect our conversations at all.

The children and I drove up that summer and Bill joined us for a briefer stay, flying up from Miami. Robert insisted that Bill drive me over to the Cancer Clinic at Dartmouth because he himself was required to have a cancer removed from his face there. He would not have known of it in time had not a physician observed it in a receiving line one evening. Since I lived in a sub-tropical climate and spent time outdoors, ergo, it was incumbent on me to seek out counsel on the damage the sun could cause. We made the lovely drive over and back to satisfy Robert.

He expressed his opinion of our daughter Mary and the Morrison daughter, Anne, as they rode off together on horseback—Mary so fair and Anne dark-eyed and brunette. He called them "prestige girls."

I had been freelancing and, therefore, was free to travel, but the next summer I signed a contract for a book that necessitated doing research in Miami, and it was proposed that sixteen-year-old Mary spend the summer visiting the Homer Noble Farm. She did, and

Ye Muirs of Florida

At Christmas 1951 a new poem

comes to you with Holiday Greetings
the warmest

from Robert Frost *of Vermont*

lest you forget him

One of many Christmas cards sent to the Muirs.

one of the events was to bang her head while riding a horse into the barn, suffering a concussion. Mary recalls the intense questioning she received each day from Robert about how she felt.

My sharpest remembrance of the 1951 visit was toward the end when we moved into the Euber farm after Larry Thompson and his family departed for Princeton.

One twilight, Robert appeared walking through the woods from his cabin carrying an unlit lantern. That night, while the children slept, Robert and I talked in front of the open fire, which he prodded from time to time.

There was no need to light the lantern because it was daylight when he left. The subjects as always were the same: God, belief, death and the eccentricities of humans.

Life goes on and then again life stops as it did for Bobby Morrison, K. and Ted's son, who was killed on his honeymoon while changing a tire.

It was a sad event for the Florida friends. Nettie Belle had designed the engagement ring for the young couple from a huge aquamarine which she describes as "half an inch long." Robert had brought it back from his Brazilian trip, the first of his overseas excursions, and had given it to Bobby to have it set.

"It was gem-stone quality," Nettie Belle remembers.

On his return to Miami after Bobby's death, Robert reported to me that Bobby's young widow had said: "Perhaps he was spared from something bad."

"Ah, no" Robert said he told her (and his eyes were soft and very kind and good, not malicious or ironic but open with kindness). "You can't do that either. You have to make it so life is good, not a bad thing to be avoided." He said it was sometimes important to insist on being "cruelly happy," a phrase he had used in a talk soon after daughter Marjorie's death.

He added: "You could throw yourself on the floor and scream and kick but the worst of it is that you always have to pick yourself up again and that is embarrassing. We don't want to go out screaming."

I wrote in my journal: "When I saw Robert for the first time on Wednesday at his house I asked how K. was.

'Fine,' he said, defying me to bring up the matter of Bobby's death.

'That's good,' I said noncommittally.

'You can either take it or go crazy,' he said.

'A lot of people are going crazy,'" I told him with a laugh.

Later, when I was leaving, he brought up the matter of Bobby to give me the details. I told him that K.'s sister had written me about it.

When I left him that day, I felt as though somebody had opened my mind and let the fresh air blow through. I felt stronger.

To capture the right word in writing was everything, just as good talk was vital with Frost, and his eagerness to act as teacher was abounding.

A decade after his death, his daughter Lesley wrote: "It was at Pinkerton Academy that my father was to discover his particular genius as a teacher. He *founded* students. To them it was revealed what it means to see, to think, to write."

Lesley was recalling that at Pinkerton Academy after the family moved to Derry Village for two years, he put on plays like Yeats' *Cathleen* and Marlowe's *Doctor*

Faustus, Lord Dunsany's *The Golden Hoop* and Milton's *Comus* while at home, Elinor and the children became lost in making costumes. For a change, Lesley's father coached baseball, his favorite sport.

This many-sided character Robert Frost began talking about writing one evening after dinner as we sat around the fire and said:

"A writer must read slowly, feeling the words, making the interpretations. In reading, the listening ear should pick up the sound and feel it in the word."

This is the individual who as a boy refused to listen to the finale of Jane Porter's *Scottish Chiefs* because he could not bear to have it end and whose daily dose of out-loud reading was as necessary as breathing out and breathing in.

That night he branched out into thoughts on freedom and equality and said that he had told the students at Spellman College to "forget about equality," which he called "mercy" and just plunge ahead with what they wanted to do—"run the race, fight the fight, write the poem or paint the picture."

When I visited Ripton on my own in the Fall of '58 Robert invited me up to the cabin and we got down to cases, as we always had.

I told him that the night before at a cocktail party given by some Harvard people I had said to the host about one of the guests: "The name Harvey Brooks means something to me. What is it?"

"It should," said our host sharply. "He's a physicist."

Robert, who had attended the party, jumped right on it. "Nonsense. Why should you know his name?" He then went on to tell me his own conversations with a Russian physicist, from Cambridge. Robert told him that "scientists were no more than exponents of 'domestic science.'"

"First," Robert told him "comes religion, made up of two parts: one superstition, the other philosophy. Next comes domestic science, which you represent, and, finally, comes gossip. Gossip is more important than any of the others. It is our way of guessing at each other."

We also talked about a preferable way to die and I posed the theory that going out on the trail like an old Indian woman, but armed with a suitable number of bottles of good whiskey might have its advantages.

Robert wondered about that particular method, but did agree that "dying out on the trail" appealed to him as well—except he "would not want to be alone."

Along with these words I wrote in my journal: "I had that lovely feeling with Robert when he cuts through to the heart of things and his impressions coincide with mine. But I am feeling now that he is increasingly frightened of old age and snatching at—what? An audience, I presume."

An amusing follow-up to "dying on the trail" occurred when K., chastising Robert for being standoffish, advised him to "stay in his cabin and be a king."

She reported to me later that he said, "But I don't want to be a king—alone."

For a parting luncheon on that visit we drove over to the Hanover Inn and sat at the outdoor cafe on a golden autumn day while Robert pointed out the very room he had occupied on the third floor of Wentworth Hall while a first-year student at Dartmouth College.

8

'THIS YOU, SHERM ADAMS?'

As *Pencil Pines* was turning into a compound, K. was observing in a letter: "It will be a puzzle to see how the place will work out with Lesley and the new Gordon house. Seems pretty much like the life I lead here. Just one set of personal relations after another."

Pencil Pines was definitely growing, but at the same time Robert was plotting a small excursion away for a less crowded piece of time in a life that increasingly was bulging with invitations and honors piling up.

K. Morrison began writing right after Christmas, proposing that she, Frost and I form a trio to go adventuring together in mid-February. "Don't tell anybody!" she warned.

Problems were preventing me from embarking on this highly desirable adventure, as I kept insisting.

Our daughter was expecting her first child, my mother had health problems and was staying with us and our twelve-year-old son enjoyed a busy schedule calling for my services as chauffeur in addition to supervision.

What got me going on this trip was that my husband was appealed to and insisted that I go.

Frost was continually "trying to get away" but again there were times when he figured out that he was "closer to people when he was all alone by himself."

So there we were, on February 15, 1958, stealing away, bound for the island of Captiva to bask in an isolated world of no telephones, a world of sea, sand and shells, a world of rare birds which we proposed to examine in their protected area.

As it turned out, we were also riding into a first-class cold front.

It hit as we were barreling through the Everglades, K. at the wheel of the rented automobile.

When the first sheet-like rains began to hit, it proved exciting. Robert began to sing *Oh Careless Love*, something he'd picked up at Bread Loaf and which he considered risqué.

I sat in the back seat, guarding the roast beef he had cooked for the expedition, while anticipating the shock that the instant mashed potatoes I planned to introduce would cause. Frost was strictly a garden fresh vegetable man. I recall that once, when we were staying at his Vermont Euber farm, I gave a pay-back picnic for which I cooked a leg of lamb. He was providing the corn on the cob from his garden, but kept postponing the delivery. He wanted the corn picked at the last minute to ensure its freshness and brought it as the first guests were arriving.

The rain had abated by the time we reached The Rod and Gun Club in the town of Everglades, where we settled in for luncheon. Here, the scene took on the ambiance of a stage set.

In that big, dark dining room on that February day there were only five guests—three of them us—and seven in help.

Our waiter was explaining that the Hollywood motion picture company making the film *Wind Across the Everglades* had just pulled out, and he had plenty to say about that. It had been exciting to see the way they lived and to have them around in what at the time amounted to a ghost town. "Still and all it was a big relief to have them gone," the waiter told us.

"They were cheap," he said, "all show people and cheap. They all came up the hard way and they were rude—like 'carny people.' Two cases of champagne in one afternoon—but no proper tips."

Is it at all possible that the stars of this wildly improbable motion picture—Burl Ives, Christopher Plummer and Gypsy Rose Lee, would be guilty as charged?

I asked the waiter if he came from Mississippi, just to keep him talking and he said, "No . . . Louisiana."

Frost was entranced, his sense of drama responding instantly to the scene. He loved the town, the dead, passed-by look of it. He suggested we have a celebratory drink before lunch.

K. said stiffly that we mustn't "make a habit of it," which made both Frost and me laugh. I realized she might be thinking back to the months after the death of Elinor when a bereaved Frost experimented with a wild assortment of drinks.

Robert explained later that he had been "out of his mind" for a full six months after his wife's death.

Before we even had touched the delicious West Coast mullet, Robert was talking about buying a place where we would all assemble "away from it all."

Frost was such a spellbinder that I could, for that moment at least, envision all of us living a free and un-interrupted life in that setting. I could see our son es-tablished in Coconut Grove's Ransom School but spend-ing weekends with us. Frost went so far as to suggest that Bill might practice law in Miami and commute!

As we left Everglades that day and continued to Captiva, Frost was asking, "Why can't a person enjoy a place without wanting to buy it?"

The arrangements for Captiva had been made with a pair of prep school teachers who had chucked the pro-fessorial life and were renting Frost a house near the Gulf with a second-story garage apartment a few feet distant from the house. K and I chose the house, where meals would be served, and Robert, the garage apart-ment.

The rains had stopped, but the cold front was mov-ing in fast. Despite that, we set out for our first walk, parading barefoot on the sandy beach, laughing and having a thoroughly good time as the temperature was dipping into the thirties.

That night, we had a rousing fire and the roast beef dinner. The magic mashed potatoes brought a reaction of amazement mixed with disgust on Frost's part. Then, after dinner, we settled down to the obligatory reading aloud. This time, Robert read the current *Newsweek*, pausing to exclaim over the various events of the world.

He kept coming back to the antics of Elsa Maxwell, party giver *extraordinaire.*

One of the most delightful things about a private evening with Frost was the variety of the conversation as he reached out into all sorts of places to find fascinating tidbits.

I remember the first time Art Buchwald was quoted to me, it was by Robert when the columnist was writing from Paris for the old *New York Herald Tribune* and his humor had caught Frost's attention.

Another tidbit that Frost picked up about then was, "If you have to tell them who you are, you're not." That came from a Walter Winchell Broadway column.

In addition to visiting a place where there were no telephones, we had come to see the birds congregate. It was freezing next day, but we spent an hour admiring egrets and herons, saw a new bird identified later as a Caspian tern. Robert and K. had visited Captiva a year before when the weather was postcard-picture perfect. They said that the press of crowds at that time made this event far superior.

After that, we turned on the car heater and crowded into the front seat to tour the island from one end to the other. We were in high spirits as we returned to the house, but entering it Robert stumbled and fell, tearing his trousers and scraping both knees. Immediately, he reacted with alarm. The right knee in particular had been giving him muscular trouble, and he paid close attention to both knees.

This was the Robert who carried from his childhood a sense of doom. K. dealt with it artfully, avoiding any suggestion of its seriousness. I dealt with it with some ointment, Band-Aids and a heating pad, which reassured him. After dinner, we were ready for a poetry reading by Robert, and the fire further helped assuage his alarms.

One evening, we decided on a bedtime walk and selected a road leading to the water, one on which automobiles traveled. As we made our way, a carload of youths came roaring along behind us, causing us to jump to the side of the road.

Robert's fury was immense as he shouted repeatedly in a way that was close to scary. It was that burning fire within, the same that brought forth love poems and those other sorrowful but always restrained poems with the inspired words.

It was that other side of Frost.

K. and I had brought along a few tasks to occupy ourselves during our stay. She was addressing envelopes for her daughter Anne's wedding while I had brought along a piece about the blind wanting to lead themselves that had been languishing too long in a file.

The next morning, after breakfast, we managed a few inroads on these. Then, at eleven o'clock, K. went over to Frost's quarters to attend to some mail, a daily ritual.

After she left I set about hard-boiling some eggs for lunch. It has already been stated that Frost considered breakfast a waste of time and further thought less of us for desiring to include it in the day's agenda. But Robert was always ready for lunch.

It happened that my eyes fell on a foot-long flow-ered lead pencil hung on a pink ribbon over the sink. On an impulse I picked it up and began writing jingles on the eggs, as I did for our children's Easter.

I had just written "This egg is for Frost / Who hates to be bossed /" when a knock on the kitchen door in-terrupted the creative process.

There stood one of our young landlords.

There I stood, hard-boiled egg and long-handled pencil in hand, while he said, "Mr. Frost is wanted on the telephone."

I was startled to hear that what had been billed as a telephone-less island actually was equipped with Alexander Graham Bell's invention and I said as much. I noticed that the young man's eyes seemed riveted on the egg and flowery pencil and wondered if he was viewing the sight as an esoteric part of a poet's life.

What he told me was that there was indeed a tele-phone secreted by a hotel executive in an automobile at the tip of the island.

Trying to decide whether to interrupt Robert and K., I found myself saying, "Well . . . it can't be much."

And then the young man was saying, "Well, it's the White House calling."

I hastened to deliver this information, and we im-mediately set forth for the tip of the island to accept the call.

In reporting on the development to Frost, I said: "At first I told the young man that you were working and I did not want to disturb you."

Robert said sternly, "Never tell them I work."

This man of passionate preference would have it that his poems floated in effortlessly—as indeed some had. He never produced a poem with a foreordained title in advance, considering that method sudden death. He preferred to "let the poem have its way" and emerge in some unexpected form.

Out of the whole incident, I carry the indelible and delicious picture of Robert Frost bending over, outside the car and reaching for the telephone inside after being told by the hotel official that it was Sherman Adams, assistant to President Dwight Eisenhower, waiting at the end of the line.

"This you, Sherm Adams?" Frost was asking in that undeniable voice. The former Governor of New Hampshire was carrying an invitation for Frost to attend a special black tie dinner at the White House on February 27.

One thing was evident: Robert Lee Frost, who got a taste of politics as a lad in San Francisco when he rode a fire engine to celebrate the election of Grover Cleveland to the presidency in a torch light parade, had picked up an appetite for the excitement of it all and had been sharpening his political skills for some time.

The funny-ness of getting away from the telephone by intent only to fall into the position of being put in touch with the White House, center of world activity— and by a car telephone, which at the time was not common procedure—was not only diverting; it was peculiarly and dramatically Frostian.

Only a month before our trip to Captiva, Robert had been presented by the Poetry Society of America with its Gold Medal for Distinguished Service at its annual banquet where a telegram from President Eisenhower was read praising "the great gifts of Robert Frost."

Sherman Adams had been responsible for the presidential greeting and just before leaving South Miami for Captiva, Robert had written to Adams suggesting it would be a fitting gesture to see that he was invited to thank the president in person. Frost actually wrote that he would welcome the idea of thanking him "at a meal."

This was information not available to me that day in Captiva, but I was well aware of the shaping of the friendship between the former governor of New Hampshire and my friend Robert.

Frost followed this up with various nudges about the importance of the arts. It was Adams who set the wheels in motion for the highly successful 1957 State Department-sponsored trip to Great Britain where Frost picked up honorary degrees of the highest importance at Oxford, Cambridge and the National University of Ireland. The latter meant much to Frost, who had acquired in boyhood the knack of perfecting an Irish brogue.

The fact is that going along with all the worldwide attention, Robert Frost was still filled with doubts as to the direction his life had taken.

He expressed them about what he called "the advertising," which, of course, he himself had set in motion. His concern about what Larry Thompson would write in the biographies after he died never left him after a certain point in the 1950s when he began to be showered with such heady attention.

One late afternoon, walking restlessly about our living room as I sat peeling potatoes for the evening meal, he paused and fixed his eyes on me.

"You never ask me for anything," he said. Then he set about filling me in on the monetary value of his manuscripts and first editions.

He appeared to hold a genuine astonishment at their value.

I listened, but could think of nothing to say.

"You never even asked me for an autograph," he persisted.

I explained that a client of Bill's had made off with our copy of the collected poems, so Bill had purchased a fresh copy.

"You had already signed it in the book store," I told Frost.

He walked over to the bookshelf and put his hand right to the copy, then demanded a pen.

Way up at the top of the page, where he had signed his name, he crossed out the "Frost," leaving the "Robert" to stand alone. Then he wrote below it: "To Helen and Bill with affection."

Finally he confronted me with a question that seemed to call for an answer.

"You never write about me anymore."

"I know," I told him, feeling helpless to provide an answer.

He said, in that deep voice for all the world like a Shakespearean actor at that moment: "You wouldn't betray me."

Why didn't I say at that time, "There is nothing to betray, Robert?" Many times I have wished that I had. It might have provided comfort to a friend who suffered more than most over a lengthy life of uncommon achievement.

The thought has come to me in the years since Robert died that in evaluating his character it might have been more generous for the scholars and critics to say that not only was Robert Frost a poet of genius but that in the twentieth century, known for its public relations, he had mastered that art and might well be called a genius in that field as well.

But in any case the memory of the trip to Captiva is a sharp and happy one.

After the call from the White House, we drove to the island grocer's, where the man who had suffered such a severe lack of money from the moment of his father's death until late in life, set about purchasing boxes of candy and culinary treats, stocked there for the affluent winter visitors. After all, he had figured that for the first forty years of his life, his total earnings from poetry did not exceed five hundred dollars.

From then on, the conversation turned to the need to catch up with his tuxedo and to make an effort to locate a hearing aid, one that fit into eye glasses perhaps. High elation was the mood of the adventuring trio as we turned back to Miami and Frost prepared to leave for the nation's capital.

Before he was done, Robert would sit down with three Presidents including Harry S. Truman and, of course, JFK at his inauguration, when he endeared himself to poets and peasants alike.

9
'A Poet In Waiting'

Frost was calling himself "a Florida farmer" but more and more he was positioning himself toward Washington, D.C.

A mere three months after President Eisenhower's invitation to dine at the White House, Robert Frost was appointed Consultant in Poetry, Library of Congress, and moved into his own private office. At once he declared in jocular fashion that he wanted to be "consulted on everything."

He was suggesting to everyone within the sound of his voice that he might care to have a go at becoming a United States Senator in order to provide insights for solving knotty problems that baffled regular politicians.

He began to refer to himself as "a poet in waiting."

Waiting for what, exactly?

He had put well behind him the island of Captiva where he had gone to "get away from it all" in favor of casting an eye on Washington political life, and meeting regularly with government officials at dinners arranged by Congressman Stewart Udall.

He was collecting captivating headlines.

The Miami Herald in one issue reported *"The United States Needs Me, Says Robert Frost."* He was having fun and the public was eating it up. Affection for this poet and formidable public figure kept on growing.

The Boston Herald was proclaiming in headlines: *"Poet—Bureaucrat Sets Dizzy Pace in Washington"* for a United Press story by a former pupil of the poet's, W.G. Rogers, in which Frost was declaring that "You have to take jealousy into account always. I'm more jealous now than I was when I was young."

He was called "the newsman's complete delight," by one observer.

But K. Morrison was writing from Cambridge in another vein.

"I'm off to Washington to get RF straightened out down there . . . the end of all this going about must be pretty soon. . . ."

What really lay ahead was more of the same for the next five years.

There was no stopping it.

All through the 1950s, honors had been piling up, none bringing more deep personal satisfaction to Robert Frost than the June 1957 State Department-sponsored trip to Great Britain.

The pageantry at Oxford where words rang with the hope that the poet would "continue to bring unfailing consolation to a suffering world" removed at least for that occasion any ambivalence in the makeup of Robert Frost.

In Ireland, posing with Prime Minister Eamon DeValera, after receiving the D. Litt. *honoris causa*, the dignity of the occasion was not lost on the American poet.

Life Magazine covered the entire pilgrimage with magnificent photographs. Particularly haunting were those depicting the tour of the old spots where he and Elinor and their children spent those happy and productive years when his first two books were published.

Lesley's daughter, Lesley Lee Francis, left her State Department job in Madrid to ride along with her grandfather on this poignant mission.

The mission was fulfilled well beyond everyone's highest hopes, but when Frost returned home he carried along with the highly prized degrees the old question, never far from his mind: How was it that he had erred so seriously in fathering his children? How did his Irish hosts with the six handsome strong sons at the dinner table all gathered together end up the way they did? It was a question that would haunt him all of his days. We talked about it over and over and one night he said: "If I'd been anything at all it should have been a Catholic."

When you think of Frost being so filled with thoughts on belief and God and constantly searching for answers, it is amazing to think of the thought tensions created by Elinor's insistence on a God-less universe and how it all contributed to the development of the poet Frost.

One evening I invited an Episcopal priest, Father Robert Martin from St. Stephen's Church, to dinner with Frost, and it turned out to be a late-late night. I was washing dishes at three a.m.

The young priest's problem was that he had an assigned sermon on "The Real Presence" and it had him up in the air trying to find a way to approach it. Robert was in his element that night, providing both answers and questions.

Frost often stated his thoughts on religion, among them "God seems to be something that wants us to win. . . . of course, somebody must lose. That's when you step up to the spiritual plane."

Talking to University of Miami students on another occasion he further declared himself.

"I assume—I believe—there is a God and that his descent into flesh was based on the principle that the supreme merit lies in risking spirit in substantiation."

Joy Reese Shaw of *The Miami Herald* was calling that occasion "one of those rare times when age and youth seem caught up in a blend of perfect harmony—in the give and take of searching and seeking."

Once Frost said: "There are not so many things in life. There is worship. Maybe that is first of all."

They were calling the 1959 winter event at the University of Miami the first Religion and Art Festival and two of the stars were Robert Frost and Philip Wylie.

Billed as an iconoclast, Wylie was not disappointing in his delivery at the Lowe Art Gallery where his topic was "Art as the Basis of Religion."

Frost and Virgil Barker at the Lowe Art Gallery in 1959.

The son of Presbyterian minister Edmund Melville Wylie was at home with his ideas, declaring the Ten Commandments "utterly inadequate" and religion a kind of "magic thinking." A rebel against Puritanism, he was blaming religion for forcing man "away from God and nature, causing him to become unnatural and anti-nature."

Robert Frost, speaking at the Plymouth Church in Coconut Grove under the auspices of the Beaux Arts of the University, was sticking to his poetry before a breathless audience, after which he was closeted in the sacristy with college students, his favorite audience.

The concept of the week's events was "to draw community and university together more closely," it was explained.

At a dinner given at Java Head, the home of the Charles Bakers, the night before the lecture at Plymouth Church, I sat with Frost on a couch waiting to be served coffee.

The pretty young lady who was attending to this rite came to us and inquired how the illustrious Mr. Frost took his coffee. He explained quietly, without inflection, a third of a cup of coffee, two thirds cream and three or four sugar tablets.

"Too much sugar isn't good for you," she told him. Maybe the word for the way she said it was "arch."

"Yeah," he said.

When she left he said, "It hasn't hurt me so far."

Frost was going his own way, eating candy by the box, cookies by the carton and four or five tablespoons of sugar in a lime drink spiked with one tablespoon of rum.

Once I stood by his side when a woman came up and gushed: "Oh Mr. Frost I just love your poem *Stopping By Woods of a Frosty Morning.*"

Before he cast a benign smile in response he shot a look of warning in my direction.

I had no intention of correcting the poor woman or breaking into laughter for that matter.

That was the night as the 1950s began when Frederick Koch directed the Robert Frost play *A Masque of Reason* in the Box Theatre of the University of Miami, a night in which Frost read some poems and enjoyed himself so thoroughly that he invited the director back to *Pencil Pines* after the show. Fred Koch remembered:

Fred Koch to right of Robert Frost with cast at the Box Theatre production of the poet's A Masque of Reason.

"We talked and talked and all of a sudden it was four a.m."

Before he departed, Frost dug up a seedling from a flowering star jasmine Koch had admired and presented it to him.

C. Clay Aldridge, the director of the Joe and Emily Lowe Art Gallery, recalls the good conversation he had with Frost during the Art and Religious Festival.

"One time I shall always remember," he wrote from his Columbus, Georgia, home, "is when Frost invited me to his cottage to show me what he did with his honorary degrees. He had a quilt made of them."

Clay recalls that Frost said: "Well, now they are of some use."

C. Clay Aldridge with Frost at the Lowe Art Gallery in 1959.

10
RF Meets the Sixties

At first he chopped his own firewood and cooked on a wood burning stove, but with the arrival of the 1960s Robert Frost decided it was time to install a fireplace.

He consulted with Bill Muir who in turn consulted with Bill Prahl and together they paid Frost a visit to discuss the project.

Prahl, the young builder grown older, remembers the pleasure associated with it and today is brimming over with recollections.

"I have such fond memories of Mr. Frost," he told me, "I was so impressed with him, his down-to-earth qualities. He was so logical. I told him my mother had an outstanding collection of orchids and he insisted that I take him to visit her.

"We rode in my jeep and he talked so entertainingly. I have six grandsons and have told every one of them all about Robert Frost."

He has a prized copy of Frost's poetry with the last seven lines of *The Wood Pile* repeated in the poet's own hand on the flyleaf. After signing it he wrote "To William Prahl with thanks for a fireplace (useful)."

The young botanist Robert Read, who had charmed Frost with his wine making, ran into trouble with that fireplace.

Frost was not charmed one bit when Read built a fire to make sure it worked.

"I cleaned it all out afterwards and even bought a set of andirons for a gift, but he was clearly annoyed. I felt it was because he had been deprived of building the first fire himself."

Frost looked Read in the eye and declared with utter firmness: "I don't want you in my private quarters."

Did the young botanist consider him a grumpy old man?

"Never. He created that image himself."

Robert Frost had been building lots of fires since leaving *Pencil Pines* in the spring for his eighty-fifth birthday splash in New York.

The dinner at the Waldorf Astoria carried weight in the area of literature due to Lionel Trilling's remarks in which he called Frost a "terrifying poet."

The political world was struck when in a morning press conference arranged by Frost's publisher, the poet came out and declared that John F. Kennedy, the junior senator from Massachusetts, might well be the next president of the United States and added that "the only Puritans left are the Roman Catholics."

The young senator had not even declared his candidacy. The press lit on the poet's prediction and Frost continued to repeat it, enjoying the attention it created.

Needless to say, JFK wrote a warm note of appreciation to the aging poet.

When Frost's term as Consultant in Poetry expired, Quincy Mumford, Librarian of Congress, invited him to stay on in a new three-year post: Honorary Consultant in the Humanities, so he remained on board, in Washington, so to speak.

Sherman Adams, who had resigned under a cloud, was lost to Frost, but he was acquiring other connections.

Frost had been involved in freeing Ezra Pound from St. Elizabeth's Hospital, where he had been languishing for all of thirteen years, charged with treason for his broadcasts from Italy in World War II.

This was a cause taken up by Archibald MacLeish and supported by Ernest Hemingway and others. Frost was brought in late, but his dramatic action helped earn the freedom of the American-born poet whom Frost had met in England on his first trip there and for whom he held no fond feelings.

As for Hemingway, when the writer killed himself, Frost took it hard. It was thought that the suicide stemmed from Hemingway's fear that he had lost his writing touch. It was something Frost dreaded for himself.

It did seem likely that Frost would continue to be enmeshed in the drama of politics.

Entering Florida, as the sixties began, there was a stopover in Gainesville for still another honorary degree, this from the University of Florida at the January 30 Commencement Convocation.

Frost accepting an honorary degree at the University of Florida.

The citation read this way:

"Robert Lee Frost, poet, teacher and wise man, your words and truths already have found their most fitting mansion, the hearts and minds of men everywhere. No academy, no institution, no society of men can pay you greater tribute than you have already received. Today we can only express, however simply and inadequately, our deep sense of thanksgiving for the way in which you and your words have revealed us to ourselves."

Frost flanked by students and Professor Villas Fernandez at a reception following the ceremony.

There were sufficient memories in Gainesville where Frost had been making friends ever since arriving in Florida and where once he and Elinor and their son Carol had driven around, scouting a permanent winter home.

The university had been sparing in awarding the degree of Doctor of Letters, *honoris causa*, the only other to have been so honored at the time being Marjorie Kinnan Rawlings. President J. Wayne Reitz was assuring the poet that he and Mrs. Reitz were planning "a small dinner" for the poet.

There was never anything small about the numbers of people attracted to Frost appearances dating back to his earliest days in Florida.

A student-writer for the college publication *The Florida Alligator* had once expressed amazement that a poet was able to converse in the area of football.

Frost told the student-writer that he had played football at Lawrence High School although he admitted that he was not a candidate for intercollegiate action.

No mention recorded here of Rob Frost's boyhood dream of becoming a famous baseball pitcher.

When invited to write a piece on his favorite sport, Frost told the readers of *Sports Illustrated*: "I never feel more at home in America than at a ball game, be it park or sandlot." He also made the comment that it was the first time he'd "met a deadline" since he was a reporter on the *Lawrence American* in 1894.

Whether in a game at Bread Loaf during the summer Vermont goings-on for writers or in the Hjort's front yard in the early 1940s in South Miami, he played to win.

Immediately after the ceremonies at the University of Florida, Frost turned his sights toward his winter refuge *Pencil Pines*. He was beginning to tell interviewers he was now "a Florida veteran."

Back at *Pencil Pines* Frost was telling Mac Smith of *The Miami News* that his favorite thing to do at *Pencil Pines* was tend to his plants, mulching and watering them, but he declared that "he'd been invited out so much" that it was interfering with his private tastes.

His private life was beginning to merge with his public life, and with much more to come in the latter.

For the moment, however, family life had taken over with the arrival of Lesley's daughter Elinor Francis Wilber and her four children.

Mac Smith attempted to draw out Douglas Wilber, aged eight, for his interview, but was firmly rebuffed.

"If you want a signature you'd better get it from my great-grandfather," he advised.

Frost was finding himself the great-grandfather of exactly eleven, one of them a namesake.

Before being photographed with the children, the poet delivered a cautionary word to photographer Joe Rimkus: "Don't make me hug them, please. I don't do hugs."

For the Public Frost there was an immediate appearance before the Friends of the University of Miami Library and, after K. arrived from Cambridge, a quick trip to Key West.

Douglas Wilber and sisters Marcia and Katherine with their great-grandfather at Pencil Pines.

Frost, Jessie Porter Newton, and K. Morrison visit on the second floor porch of Heritage House in Key West.

Frost was back in the nation's capital in May, testifying before a Senate subcommittee, amid gratifyingly large audiences, declaring that what the nation needed was a National Academy of Culture. He was telling the committee that his dearest wish was to see poetry given equal time with scholarship and science.

The poet said something familiar: ". . . All art is performance. It is not scholarship," and concluded, "I do want you to declare our equality. We will take care of the rest."

The next month, the Senate passed a bill awarding a gold medal to Frost "in recognition of his poetry, which has enriched the culture of the United States and the philosophy of the world." It was sent to President Eisenhower after the House of Representatives did its part and passed into law by mid-September.

Unfortunately, there was a temporary hitch: Congress had forgotten to appropriate the money for the Frost medal.

Frost was out lecturing in the West that Fall and it was in Los Angeles that he learned of JFK's election to the presidency. It was he, not Eisenhower, who would present the gold medal to Frost, who held high hopes that the new young president would pay even closer attention to the arts.

The hope was realized almost immediately when JFK appointed Stewart Udall his secretary of the Interior. At once, the new cabinet member, who had followed Sherman Adams as the poet's personal political guide, made the suggestion that Robert Frost should play a role in the inauguration.

The new president was not entirely sure at first, being totally aware of the possibility that the old bard might steal his show.

On that cold snowy day in the nation's capital on January 20, 1961, Robert Frost provided a dramatic warmth that amounted to a throat-catcher for the nation.

Not un-dramatic was the invitation issued to visit the First Lady and the new president at eleven o'clock the next morning and being received in their bedroom.

This was surely a time for chanting the Kipling line, "If only my mother could see me now."

11
'DON'T FORGET ME'

When Robert Frost shed the snows of the Washington Inauguration and arrived back at *Pencil Pines* on January 29, 1961, he had dinner with Marie and Donald Gordon, then telephoned us.

He was asking would I be taking him to receive the honorary degree at the University of Miami scheduled for a few days away?

By then I was pretty tied up with "the arts" which Frost had been ballyhooing so spectacularly and it developed that I would be reviewing a play and could not even attend the ceremony, let alone escort him.

A call to our mutual friend, C. Doren Tharp, provided the more than willing and welcome escort. Doren was vice president of the university and better equipped for the charge than I, as a matter of fact.

That winter was becoming crowded.

Increasingly there were less and less opportunities for quiet conversations with our friend Robert. He had been complaining about there being too much going on a year before in that interview in *The Miami News*.

Frost receiving an honorary degree from the University of Miami.

Looking back on the winter of '61 what stands out is the memory of a three-way talk with Frost and Fred Shaw, who taught writing at Miami-Dade Community College which led to the post of becoming book editor of *The Miami Herald.*

Fred and I had become good friends after he rescued me by covering the first Shakespeare Festival at the University of Miami when our daughter starred in at least three plays.

Despite the opinion of managing editor Jim Bellows of the *News* that I should act as critic for these productions, I wisely refused on the grounds that it would test the mother-daughter relationship to an untenable extent. So I literally hired Fred to write the reviews.

We talked a lot about Ireland that night and Robert took pleasure in twitting me about my Irish roots in the playful mode that he maintained in public but it was all warm and pleasurable. It was a distinct pleasure bringing Frost and Fred Shaw together and joining in the talk.

That was the winter that the Friends of the University of Miami Library brought Max Wylie down from New York to speak and his brother Phil and Ricky planned a warm welcome in the form of a cocktail party for forty.

We all gathered at the appointed time but regrettably Max was not able to make it, being snowbound in New York. He did, however, arrive in time to give the talk on Eugene O'Neill, the playwright, next day as scheduled. It was an event we had all been anticipating—but I didn't make that occasion either.

It all coincided with the period of my fiftieth birthday and the Wylies planned a celebration for me. I had been baking birthday cakes for Phil and Ricky for years while Ricky baked Bill's and mine.

The 1961 birthday party also went on without me but those who attended, including Frost and K. Morrison, who arrived from Boston in time, saved the cake for the birthday child.

I had already blown out candles on a cake that read "Viva Mama," in the presence of husband, daughter and first grandson, Barney Lindsley, while lolling in bed with a fever.

The following day after his lecture, Max Wylie presented himself in my boudoir with flowers and gave me the gist of his talk on O'Neill. The Wylie sister, Verona Slater, who had come from Sarasota for all these celebrations, presented me with the Wylie birthday cake. My room was a bower of flowers.

Robert chose chocolates to send to the ailing member of the Muir family and followed it up with an invitation to dine with him at El Dorado after recovery set in.

Bill and Mary and I had that leisurely dinner with him before he left that winter. He was preparing for his trip to Israel and Greece, both of which proved rewarding events for him, but when he landed in London with more commitments he called a halt.

He said he was not feeling well and the London physician agreed that he should return to Vermont at once.

In August 1961 K. Morrison was writing from Ripton about Robert's early return from the trip to Israel and Greece and the attendant complications of visitors "Lesley, Granddaughter Robin, Udalls, Untermeyers" and declaring: "I think you will see a great change in RF. So it seems to me."

The opportunity to observe this did not occur until the following February.

The first inkling I had that Frost had arrived in Miami was when Bill tracked me down at a meeting to say that K. was trying to reach me from Cambridge. Robert had arrived at *Pencil Pines* and was reporting in sick over long distance, then hanging up because he had trouble hearing. When she asked if he had talked to me he said mournfully, "Helen doesn't care if I live or die."

I hurried over to *Pencil Pines* where I realized at once a medical opinion was needed and put in a call for our friend Dr. Franz Stewart, Sr. When he arrived and examined Robert he concluded that, considering his age, the proper place for him would be the hospital.

Robert's eyes pleaded as he turned to me. The doctor caught it and asked if there was anybody who could stay with him that night, that he should not be left alone.

Robert put his silent request into words. Could I spend the night?

He had a deep-seated cold but had been wary of my calling the doctor. At the same time he was struck with the fear of pneumonia, the old bugaboo.

I realized his need and said that I'd call Bill and check on things. Toby was away at school, Mary was married and, of course, Bill said "stay."

I drove home and picked up a few overnight needs and went by the drug store for prescriptions ordered by the doctor. When I got back to Robert's he assured me that he would definitely throw up the pills—and later delivered on the promise.

Getting the lights doused for the night was a problem. Sick or well, Robert wanted to converse. He kept appearing in the small hallway between the bedroom and sitting room and stood surveying the makeshift bed I had arranged on the couch.

Getting Robert to take the pills had been something of a task. Early in our friendship he had advised me to "every day have one small victory." When he downed the pills, I assured him that it was my "small victory for February 1, 1962."

He wanted to know about all of us and, finally, I said if he would return to bed I would fill him in.

The only moment Robert was at all relaxed that night was when I told him that Toby had written from school that he had spent a Sunday afternoon lying in his bunk reading Frost poetry.

I wrote Toby later, "Robert said, 'That pleases me, to know that Toby was readin' me.' He said it to show that not too much real pleasure came from the fat public life, the spotlight life, but only in individual instances."

It turned out that night that Robert had a lot on his mind.

He had not been as happy as usual in Decatur, Georgia at Agnes Scott College because he had been asked what he considered an overly rude question: Did he think that poetry was going out of fashion?

It inflamed him and he responded hotly.

Years before he had told me that if he ever said one thing in a talk that displeased him, "that night I do not sleep."

Finally, he got to the real burden he was carrying: Lesley had told him in New York as he started south that she intended selling the house she and Joe Ballantine had built on Robert's acreage.

What would Bill, as Robert's Florida lawyer, think about that?

I kept trying to downplay that as something that might not come to pass and began bringing up happy pieces of information. I felt that Robert was purposely making himself sick by brooding over family matters.

What about the plans afoot to create the Robert Frost Memorial park in Ripton and the truly happy occasion of the recent dedication of the Robert Lee Frost Elementary School in Lawrence, Massachusetts, the town from which his father had fled and to which his wife and children were forced to return after his death for family assistance?

That honor was free of political engineering and therefore pure enough to suit the heart of a poet.

Troubling to him that night was the old question of "too much advertising." He wondered about the March 30th issue of *Life* Magazine, scheduled to carry his picture on the cover. Wasn't it going too far?

We got through the night, and in the morning the daytime practical nurse sent by Dr. Stewart arrived while I set forth to market in order to stock up on the proper foods for the patient.

I also had to arrange to cancel an appointment for an interview with Tennessee Williams.

It was a peculiar situation, my not being able to tell the newspaper I worked on (I was serving as drama critic of *The Miami News* during the period) about the distinguished patient I was attending because it would have opened journalistic complications.

I decided to take Editor Bill Baggs into my confidence and he agreed to hold up on any story until I gave the signal.

Not unexpectedly, Robert proved to be a difficult patient.

He exhibited a marked tendency to run his own show, down to insisting on eating out of the icebox, refusing trays, walking about the house—and once plunging outdoors, with the nurse in hot pursuit.

Nevertheless, he was in safe hands with Dr. Stewart, and things went along comfortably for days with me bringing fish chowder and other tempting offerings while up in Cambridge, K. Morrison prepared to move up her arrival date.

There was a miscalculation on my part the day I brought our grandson Barney to visit, on the grounds it would divert Robert.

Frost was in no mood to share my attentions with this four-year-old, so we left promptly and I returned unencumbered.

The doctor made tests that proved Frost had no deep infection, just the virus, and his heart was OK. Despite that, he was convinced that he had pneumonia and went on worrying.

The day came when the doctor gave permission for a modest stroll, and Robert turned it into something else, getting his feet wet and claiming he was "sicker."

The nurse reached me in the City Room to say that "Mr. Frost was carrying on" and telephoning K. to tell her that if she and Alfred Edwards, his publisher, "cared to see him alive they'd better get down to Florida fast."

I drove to *Pencil Pines* and assured Robert that K. would be arriving in two days time and that Al Edwards had booked a flight for the seventh.

Nothing would console him. In the early morning he became worse, his temperature rose and he had a shaking chill and cough with bloody sputum. This suggested pneumonococus pneumonia.

A change came over Robert as he bent to the inevitable. He began calling me "dear," urging me "not to get too close because of the germs," handing me a gardenia he'd placed on his bedside table.

While we waited for the ambulance he gave me a sacred charge: I was to guard his satchel of poems, his body of work so to speak, although God forbid I should use such a word for his poetry.

We saw Robert off in the ambulance with the nurse and I followed in Dr. Stewart's car. It was a low moment. We almost had kept Frost out of the place he dreaded and were it not for his willfulness, would have done so.

When we arrived at Baptist Hospital the doctor disappeared upstairs and I was faced with Admissions. The woman had no idea Robert was of any consequence as she asked the usual questions.

When she got to the question "Religion?" I hesitated. How did you answer "none" to one of the most religious persons ever born? I said, "No formal affiliation."

When I told him about it later, he said: "You should have told her I was an Old Testament Christian." It was a phrase he and his rabbi friend Victor Reichert had concocted.

Later, I gave the line to Bill Baggs, who used it in a column. It was a thank-you for holding up on the story.

I let Baggs know immediately, of course, by calling from the hospital to keep my end of the bargain and inform him that Robert was once again back in the public eye.

After the news of the Frost illness was flashed over the wires I could explain to Tennessee Williams why I had been forced to cancel our interview. We had luncheon in Coconut Grove, after which the playwright sent the poet magnificent long stemmed roses to the hospital.

The medical story as gleaned from Dr. Stewart all these years later involves a middle-of-the-night decision on his part when he went by to check on his patient and discovered that in addition to pneumonia the heart rhythm had become too fast and irregular. Penicillin had been started the night before.

He explained that the penicillin was taking care of the pneumonia but other medication was required and he wondered if Frost could swallow a capsule?

"Certainly," Robert told him and the doctor scurried down to the pharmacy to have what amounted to four pills placed in the capsule, which was downed by his patient without protest.

It is generally agreed that the treatment at three a.m. put the poet back in circulation and as usual with a quip.

A doctor at the hospital told him that pneumonia was considered the "old man's friend," and Frost replied: "What does that make penicillin to me?"

The day he was dismissed from the hospital Frost insisted on stopping by Nettie Belle Hjort and Dr. John Robinson's new home to check it out and walked around the grounds, inspecting the planting. He was still wearing his pajama top, Nettie Belle observed.

Rest was required for a few weeks, but he was soon able to plunge into the plans for the publishing of his new book, *In the Clearing*, being rushed for his March 26th eighty-eighth birthday bash in Washington.

Months later, back in Ripton, Robert remembered his Florida doctor and sent an autographed copy of *In the Clearing* with these words: "To Franz Stewart who miraculously pulled me through, for this and more too I begin to hope since the strength I felt in the Crimea." He signed it: "Robert Frost of Ripton, Vermont when not in Florida," and dated it September 26, 1962. As a postscript under the date he added "and for Ruth and her music as of obligation unforgettable."

Mrs. Stewart had invited Jean Bedetti, the retired first cellist with the Boston Symphony, to play shortly after Frost's recovery. The pair had formed a mutual admiration society, each insisting the other was the greater artist.

Robert hit on an amazing farewell scene by calling me into his "private quarters" with the new fireplace that Bill Muir and Bill Prahl had conspired to put into place.

I found myself sitting down facing him across a desk. He said he "wanted to thank me for all I had done."

I had never seen my friend Robert sitting behind a desk before. Instead of a desk, he had all through his life manufactured a writing lapboard of cardboard to which he attached a pencil on a string.

The whole scene was peculiarly official-sounding and utterly unlike any other shared moment. I felt awkward. I think he did too.

I stood up to terminate the conversation. Neither of us spoke.

Then he said, "Don't forget me."

I waited to find words, then said: "Not likely" and laughed.

As we walked across to the other cottage I found my head ringing with the words "Good-bye, good-bye to everything."

It was the Robert Louis Stevenson poem that the children found pleasure in called *Farewell to the Farm*.

As I left *Pencil Pines* that day the words from the last lines floated in and out of my head: "Crack goes the whip, and off we go / The trees and houses smaller grow . . ."

I felt strongly that day that I was saying good-bye to *Pencil Pines*.

And so I was.

12

Up, Up and Away . . .

There was no hesitation in the way Robert met his eighty-eighth birthday bash, the like of which had not been seen before for any poet, American or otherwise.

It all began with a Washington press conference in which he praised Eisenhower, calling him "a friend" and followed that remark by referring to Nikita Khrushchev, the Soviet Premier, as "a grand man."

"He's my enemy" the poet admitted, "but it takes just a little magnanimity to admire him."

How's that for gathering headlines?

Next on the agenda was a White House ceremony when President Kennedy presented Frost with the gold medal awarded under the Eisenhower administration.

So it was that JFK was the president to receive the first copy of *In the Clearing* with a flowery autograph that began "Great circumstances have raised this book to be more yours, O my president, yours and your lady's than it is the lady's who made me make it."

That lady would be Kathleen Morrison and at the birthday dinner that night Robert closed the after-dinner remarks by referring to her again as his "devoted secretary for more than twenty years."

The salutes to the poet were so lengthy that it was five minutes after midnight before he rose to speak. He held the attention of the two hundred people gathered that night for twenty-five minutes. Those who praised Robert Frost included such luminaries as Chief Justice Earl Warren, Adlai Stevenson and poets Mark Van Doren and Robert Penn Warren

The old bard was proving himself to be indestructible.

Publisher Al Edwards had planned every detail of the extravaganza and had taken the gamble of printing an unprecedented fifty thousand copies of *In the Clearing* issued for the poet's birthday.

It proved to be not too great a gamble.

The advance sale alone hit twenty-seven thousand and Edwards felt secure in the fact that he was heading toward one-hundred thousand.

Frost had smashed all records for the sale of poetry since 1895, when record taking began.

This refuted the *New York Times* assertion that "forty years of modernism had left the public disenchanted with poetry."

Al Edward's explanation of the Frost success went like this: "Frost is known out there as a man of wisdom. The public knows him. Taxi drivers sometimes recite his own poetry to him."

The *Life Magazine* spread with Robert Frost's picture on the cover referred to him as "America's ageless poet."

Inside there were "Seven Poems from his Wonderful New Book." Jackie Kennedy's "dazzling trip" to India, also announced on the cover, took second billing.

He would fly higher and higher before he was done.

When he heard that Stewart Udall, his introducer to the world of Washington following the departure of Sherman Adams, was scheduled to travel to Russia, he listened. And when invited to the Udall home for an evening with Anatoly Dobrynin, the Russian Ambassador, he was elated.

The evening ended with Udall suggesting that an exchange of poets between the United States and the Soviet Union would be appropriate.

The wheels began to turn for planning this event.

Frost had determined that, in addition to traveling under the State Department auspices, what he would prefer, in order to authenticate the mission, would be a personal word from President Kennedy and he achieved it.

The story of the trip to Russia was told in front-page headlines and to soften his campaign to achieve it, Robert described himself as "an opportunist on the loose . . ."

Make no mistake about it, he wanted to be part of politics, and having it come so late in life did nothing to lessen the gleeful satisfaction.

There can be no doubt in the minds of anybody who knew the story of Robert Frost's early days in San Francisco with his ambitious and politically failed father that his son's appetite for political intrigue was formed and solidified way back then.

Robert was only six years old when his father was elected to travel to Cincinnati as a member of the California delegation of Democrats to work toward the nomination of General Winfield Scott Hancock as a candidate for president.

The excitement of seeing his father depart for this event was never forgotten; nor was the disappointment when General Garfield won out over Hancock for the nomination.

Imagine the satisfaction the famous poet received when he sat down at a small dinner party next to former President Harry Truman to hear him say that Hancock should have won that nomination.

William Frost's struggle for political power did not end with that campaign, however. When he ran for tax assessor of San Francisco, his son, then ten years old, was by his side. Sometimes he wished his father's street talks were a bit more colorful in order to grab attention.

That was 1884, with Grover Cleveland filling the Democratic ticket for president. The boy Rob distributed handbills, ran errands, and filled himself with free lunches at the saloons.

Never lost to him was the memory of the torchlight parades and the time sparks fell on his own head, and when he rode in a float and delivered messages for his father to City Hall.

When William Prescott Frost, Jr., had quit his newspaper job to devote himself to running for office, he was certain of winning. When he lost, it was a blow from which he never recovered. He stayed away from home for days after election night, continuing the long established heavy drinking. His health deteriorated quickly, and when he died in the spring of 1885 he left his family penniless, dependent on his father back in Massachusetts, to send money for tickets to travel there.

In the end, the rebel son had asked to be buried back home in New England.

Now in the autumn days of 1962 his son was about to ride an airplane to the Soviet Union as an important representative of his government.

I was in New York that October of 1962 to welcome our first granddaughter into the world and at the same time review the Broadway plays. I spent a bit of time with Lesley.

Robert's trip had splashed headlines all over the world, but the most provocative was one he would gladly have traded.

Stepping off the airplane on the arm of Stewart Udall and exhausted from the trip, he faced a battery of the press and the adroit maker of phrases slipped up and put words into the mouth of Khrushchev that he himself had contrived.

He said that the Russian had declared that America would prove "too liberal to defend itself," as next day's *Washington Post* pointed out.

It was the end of cordiality between President Kennedy and the man named for the Confederate hero, Robert E. Lee.

All this had already happened when Lesley and I were meeting in New York. I sat in her high ceilinged East Tenth Street apartment and experienced an ominous sense of dissolution, mainly because of the accumulation of family papers, for all the world like a musty library.

I was preparing to leave by automobile with Ricky Wylie for Florida, and Lesley saw me to the street where we stood on a cold Fall day and found ourselves in a warm embrace.

We had never been close friends but that day we were and with plenty of unsaid things between us.

When I came down with a strep sore throat and had to board a train for the last leg of the trip home I wondered about all the military presence.

Lesley had asked whether I'd be seeing her father in Washington and I told her I wasn't sure. It turned out that Frost would be there addressing the National Poetry Festival and hoping to redeem himself for the Khrushchev remarks. When the White House reception for the poets was canceled, Frost feared the uproar he had caused was responsible for the cancellation.

What we did not know that day was that the Cuban Missle Crisis was the prime interest of President Kennedy. Not until I arrived in Miami and saw the military buildup closer up did I have an inkling of what was happening. It was made clear when President Kennedy made his announcement to the nation.

The chat between the poet and the premier was an unpleasant reality for the president of the United States at a delicate period in the nation's history.

It would have seemed appropriate to rest after the demanding trip to Russia. Instead, an agenda that would have shaken a younger man was pursued as Frost traveled to New York with K. accompanying him to receive the MacDowell Colony Medal.

There President Kennedy *did* send a telegram but it did not constitute the personal touch that Robert craved.

Dartmouth and Amherst claimed him and at the latter college, a piece of good news was that a gift amounting to 3.5 million dollars was earmarked for a library in his name.

Frost kept appointments all over the country, and at the fiftieth anniversary of *Poetry Magazine*, where his early poetry had been recognized, he made an admission that he actually liked cities. "I knew very well I would not sell my poetry in the country," he told his audience.

Once, he and Elinor had taken an apartment in New York for a month and he had tried to get a newspaper job on the *New York Sun*. He had been turned down.

His last hurrah occurred on December 2 when he addressed the Ford Hall Forum in Boston and ended his talk with a puzzling remark.

"It's a wonderful world," he said. "To hell with it."

His last audience was mystified.

The next day he entered Peter Bent Brigham Hospital in Boston, but not surprisingly K. had a bit of trouble at convincing him it was necessary.

Days before, the sad news had arrived that Stafford Dragon, who ran the farm operations at the Homer

Noble Farm in Ripton, had lost his son Richard in an automobile accident. This meant that the Morrisons were obliged to attend the funeral.

After showing signs of rebellion about entering the hospital Frost gave in and assured K. he would conduct himself "on the highest plane."

He kept his word.

His daughter Lesley's three-day visit occurred immediately and when his condition improved she returned to her duties in New York, leaving K. Morrison and her daughter Anne in charge.

The medical diagnosis was chronic cystitis. There was surgery, followed by recoveries, more surgery and in the end the prognosis was that the long life of the poet was drawing to a close.

When that day came, the doctors opened the doors for important visitors who, after clearance, stood in line to pay their respects.

Russian poets brought champagne and the titled daughter of Ezra Pound brought thanks to the suite that had earlier been occupied by King Ibn Saud of Saudi Arabia.

On January 5, Frost received the Bollingen prize and the words of gratitude pouring from his lips were directed toward his peers, his doctors and his friends—and the whole world for that matter.

It was a gratifying manner in which to leave the world, considering the way he had entered it.

On that March day in San Francisco the physician who arrived to deliver the first child of Belle Moodie and William Prescott Frost, Jr., faced an armed father-to-be. Placing a pistol on a table, he assured the doctor that there must be no slip-up in the delivery of this child or he would have to answer for it.

Never an absence of drama in the life of Robert Lee Frost.

Even as his life ebbed, the habit of forming words never died. He was working on a poem in the hospital days before the end, which came January 29, 1963.

Friends in Miami were aware of the impending death and long distance calls were part of that night.

I turned off the light at two a.m. and at exactly four a.m. the telephone rang. I was being called to *The Miami News* to write a sidebar on page one for the street edition telling of the death of one of the city's most celebrated winter residents.

I dressed quickly and obliged and was surprised to find it wrote itself. The sense of deep loss would come later.

13
GOING TO SEE ROBERT

I had to weigh the reasons for keeping my promise to review Moliere's *Tartuffe* at the University of Miami's Ring Theatre or accept the invitation to attend the Robert Frost Memorial Service at Amherst College on February 17, 1963, at two p.m. The reserved seat would be held until 1:50 p.m., after I sent my acceptance.

Editor Bill Baggs, who had held back the story on the poet's grave illness for me a year earlier, made the decision that I go and, furthermore, file a story for Miami readers.

Amherst is not the most accessible location and it was zero weather and snowing. I got a reservation for a flight to Springfield, Massachusetts, with a change in Newark, New Jersey.

There I ran into Rabbi Victor Reichert, Robert's good friend, and we sat together talking about Robert all the way to Springfield.

I told the Rabbi that on the flight from Miami I had suddenly realized that my brain was supplying words for the humming of the airplane engines. *Going To See Robert* is what the engines were telling me.

I confided that I always felt that Robert had chosen me for a friend. Immediately, the Rabbi said he had the exact same feeling.

I suppose all over there are people like that.

One Thanksgiving Robert had taken the Rabbi's place as a preacher for his Cincinnati congregation. There was no way Rabbi Reichert would not be present at this service.

Dignitaries were arriving by the plane load, flying in on a special flight from Washington to Westover Air Force Base.

Hundreds came with less comfort from all over America, at some personal cost. Not all were celebrated.

A black railroad porter from Boston's Back Bay Station, James Canaday, was present. After Frost's serious illness in Miami in 1962 this man had traveled to New York from Boston to smooth the path of the poet after his ride up from Florida.

There were plenty of the celebrated, of course. Chief Justice Warren and his wife arrived at historic Johnson Chapel, the spot Robert Frost had chosen for his wife's memorial service because it was "beautiful" despite her non-religious insistence.

The hour-long service brought India's B.K. Nehru to the Chapel along with important government figures, many judges, writers and poets. The high-ceilinged, sunny room filled to its capacity of seven hundred while others watched over closed-circuit television from other college buildings.

Alvin H. Plimpton, Amherst's president, said: "Now he is missing. I cannot speak for his poetry though it does speak to me. His poetry is with us, but what I will miss is the man.

"His voice carried without wires; his vision, further than television. Since 1916 he would come and stand here.... You never felt you knew a little of Robert Frost, and no one ever knew him all. The part you knew was given to you with such intensity—the part you saw was so vivid—that while his poetry belongs to the ages, Frost the man and the teacher belongs to us."

Mark Van Doren read Frost poetry. Chosen to give the invocation was another Frost friend, the Reverend Henry Wise Hobson, Bishop of the Episcopal Diocese of Southern Ohio. He told the assembled friends of Robert Frost that "his search for truth was constant and unwavering.... He believed that the source of all truth is God and the passion of his life was to discover more truth."

There was scarcely a hint of death in the entire ceremony and the celebration begun the night before continued at the Lord Jeffrey Inn, where friends gathered for dinner and to talk about the poet.

"He slept late," one said, "to avoid having to eat breakfast." All the dear and pleasant things were called up for this moment of farewell.

I filed a story for *The Miami News* and ended it this way: "Dr. Lawrance Thompson of Princeton University, a close friend and official biographer of the poet, said it quite simply over coffee: 'This is a love feast.'"

In the light of what Larry's biographies would suggest, one could only wish some of that love had echoed in the words he wrote.

The final poem read by Van Doren was *I'm Bound Away*, in which the poet advised his friends to "go get well wined" when his time came to depart this earth.

I used it in the beginning of my own *Miami News* story, which I put on the wire immediately after the service before joining my daughter Mary and other friends at the Lord Jeffrey Inn for more conviviality.

When we all said good-bye and went our separate ways a good friend of Robert's, Howard Schmitt of Hamburg, New York, offered to drive me to Albany to catch a plane for my return to Miami, where various deadlines awaited me. We talked about Frost and it was all happy talk.

On my arrival in Miami almost the first thing I did was open the newspaper to check the story I'd written.

To my horror one of the poet's words was transformed and came out this way: "Let my friends get well *winded* and go lie down."

Whether to lay this error on Western Union or a composing room operator was not the point.

The point—and a sharp one indeed—was that this represented the first of many times when I would wish to share a bit of ironic laughter with this extraordinary friend.

I knew then that the friendship, like the poetry, would not die, but the lovely black laughter was gone forever.

14

AFTER THE ABYSS

In September of 1964 Lesley Frost flew into steamy Miami from sunny Spain and the twenty-five room house she had bought for a small girl's school on the grounds of La Granja Castle in the Village of San Ildefonso, five miles out of Segovia. She was busily packing books and furnishings from her recently sold South Miami house while we talked.

A heavy schedule of lecturing on "Education by Poetry" lay ahead. She explained that there would be no anecdotes relating to her childhood.

"I avoid the personal," she told me, "and talk about Father's poems, what they mean to me, what they mean to everybody."

Two of her granddaughters, Marcia and Katherine Wilber, were students in the small school. Actually Lesley had started with them in mind after they expressed a wish to travel abroad.

Lesley was busy with lectures and family matters while perpetuating her father's poetry in a number of ways. But she had time to discuss politics.

The daughter of the poet who appeared, white hair flying in the wind, at the inauguration of the young

Democratic president, had this to say: "I am a Goldwater fanatic."

My review of *Selected Letters of Robert Frost* by Dr. Lawrance Thompson had just appeared in a spread in the August 30, 1964, Florida Living section of *The Miami News* and under a large photograph the editor had written "Robert Frost: Massive and Mischievous, Proud and Ambitious, a Complicated Character of Letters."

Nobody could quarrel with that, but before my review copy arrived I had had a letter from K. Morrison. She was writing from Cambridge to say "Larry's *Selected Letters* are out—not yet, but I have the first copy. They are what he said they would be—an ice breaker for the biography. Marvelous and strange they are. . . . What bothers us is that though Larry says nothing but the truth in his little preamble to each letter, his sense of language is somewhat limited, with the result that he makes his statement sound very stark and very hard.

"Then he uses a word that has the wrong overtone. . . . Ted says it is almost as if Larry had a grudge against Robert . . . but very subtle. . . ."

It is no surprise that the Harvard English professor should have been the first to catch the undercurrents in the Thompson approach to his subject.

When Theodore Morrison met his wife, Scottish-born Kathleen Johnston, a clergyman's daughter, back in the Twenties, he was serving as an editor of the *Atlantic Monthly*, where she was employed. It was after their marriage and he had joined the Harvard faculty that K. embarked on re-setting the course of Robert Frost's life following his wife's death.

When Ted died in the late eighties he had contributed a number of novels, translated the *Viking Portable Chaucer,* and wrote poetry in addition to teaching at Harvard.

Others would be slower to pick up the thread that would result in the volumes of biography causing the altering of the Frost image.

Lesley was in Spain running her school in 1970 when the second volume of Thompson's biographies, *Robert Frost: The Years of Triumph 1935-1938,* was published, so her letter of shock arrived later than the flood of protests that reached the *New York Times* after their reviews appeared.

When her letter did appear in *The Times* it had a telling message and touched on the family theme.

"Far from being a 'disastrous family life,' ours was a splendid one. . . . struck too often by tragedy—but tragedy is something else again from evil."

She called her father "a creative genius" with his "own worst enemy, doubt of himself. . . ."

Lesley kept in close touch with our family as time went on, being certain to send invitations for all the events she worked to bring about, such as the restoration of the Derry Farm in New Hampshire and the plaza named for her father in San Francisco, always keeping us up to date with clippings.

When *The Family Letters of Robert and Elinor Frost* came out in 1972, I had just returned from San Francisco and found Lesley had been telephoning.

I wrote her a note which included this paragraph: ". . . I finally got the *Family Letters*—they were pokey about sending it—but it was worth waiting for. My feeling is that the RF I see in the *Family Letters* was the RF I knew. It wasn't until 1941 that we became friends so I missed knowing your mother and I regret that.

"The Muir-Frost friendship was deep and intimate and it fit in someplace between public and family, which I suppose is why I am so often offended by some of the things written about your father."

I was also telling Lesley that we regretted being unable to attend the memorial service for Joe Ballantine being held at the Bennington Cemetery on June 1, 1973.

In February 1976, Lesley was writing at length to say how tired she was as she approached her seventy-seventh birthday—and hoping she could visit Miami before she went to the San Francisco ceremony to mark her father's birthday anniversary in March.

The family theme went on as she told us where each grandchild was and what each was doing and then she said this touching thing:

"I am under the pressure of things that have to be done (or ought to be and are an excruciating mental handicap) before the light goes off. The demands of schools, of libraries, of researchers, of just individuals writing doctorates, of the Derry farm. . .

"I have recently been up to see Irma—something I do several times a year. She stays the same and is so well cared for she will outlive us all—and is another drain on my emotions. . ."

Robert Frost's daughter, Lesley, the year of her mother's death when she was thirty-nine. She had her father's eyes.

Lesley was declaring the need for a "talk of talks" with us but it would be three years before she made it back to accomplish it.

When it happened she sat in a corner of the porch on the straw settee her father had occupied so many times and used the word he had uttered over and over, the word he used instead of death: the "abyss."

She looked like him. They had the same arresting blue eyes. Her attachment to metaphor in all those lectures that occupied her were the result of those early years when she called her father Rob and decided that he was "pretty good at this metaphor game."

When I heard her use the word "abyss" to describe death I was swept more than ever into the family story of Elinor and Robert Frost.

It was about the time of the year when her father was accustomed to arrive for his winter stay in South Florida.

What I said to her that day was "I wish Robert could be here with us. I think we could all talk contentedly together today."

Lesley smiled a sad-sweet smile and said, "I think we could . . . today."

We sat without words, looking out over the rose apple tree. "When you are little they tell you about fairies and magic . . . when you're old they're still covering up sickness," she said sadly.

She began to speak about how *Stopping By Woods of a Snowy Evening* was written. "He was carrying eggs to the village to sell in order to get money for Christmas presents," she said somberly.

I told her that Robert had once told me that *The Road Not Taken* stemmed from a walk with his best friend of a lifetime, the English writer Edward Thomas, and had to do humorously with which road to take on one of their deeply satisfying walks together during that idyllic period of Lesley's girlhood.

Lesley was telling me, "My father was not motivated by ambition. It was poetry. But he was also motivated by fear from childhood—fear of Chinese children who chased him. . . . and of his father. . ."

And then about Carol: "My father tried to cure him of fear and all he did was make him more fearful."

The date of this conversation was February 1, 1979, a year before Bill died, and I thought so much of it that I went instantly and wrote it down. Lesley died in 1983.

That day I said to her: "You were alike in some ways."

Lesley answered: "My father said: 'How can you admire my poetry and be so critical of me?'"

In spite of their differences there was a closeness that showed in the final notes they exchanged as he lay dying.

"I think of you as Robert Coeur de Lion," she told him and he dictated back these words: "You are something of a Lesley de Lion yourself . . . You can't know how much I have counted on you in family matters . . . "

I asked Lesley that day, which turned out to be a final disclosure sort of thing, about how it worked, with her mother being an agnostic and her father so deeply committed to searching for God.

She had a ready answer and indeed wrote a splendid and revealing essay to introduce *New Hampshire's Child* about that very thing.

Lesley said "my mother was pure goodness and her spirituality was elemental, a thing in itself."

In the essay, Lesley wrote, "In contrast, my father tended toward self pity. He was given to self torture, even taking a certain pride in the idea that God had somehow planned to give him a hard time. There was Job, wasn't there?"

I could hear her father's voice saying: "It's all right with me, if it's all right with God."

In my review of that book, in *The Miami Herald,* I wrote: "An ambiance, gray and ghostlike, attends the flower picking, the tree climbing and star gazing. . . .

"With any help from the reader's imagination the Journal, augmented by the notes, assumes the shape of a dramatic play with O'Neill overtones. One puts down the book, grateful that the Frost poems do not change and do not die."

End Word

It is today's fashion to strip: on stage, on film and certainly after death to tear away every shred of protective garment from the characters we honor in life.

The more honor bestowed in life, the greater abuse heaped on the individual after death seems to be the way of it.

Nothing new about it. Back in 1923 in a *New York Times* interview Robert Frost was exclaiming about this tendency.

He told a writer named Rose C. Feld: "I hear people speak of men who are writing today, and their eyes light up with a deep glow of satisfaction when they can mention some putrid bit of gossip about them. 'He writes such lovely things,' they say, and in the next breath add, half worshipfully, 'He lives such a terrible life.'"

At the time, Robert had earned his first Pulitzer, was winding up a two-year stint at the University of Michigan and was on the eve of returning to Amherst to continue teaching, doing it his way and at the same time figuring out how best to make his way as a poet.

He made it to the very top leaving behind a trail of words.

The tone of irony appears and reappears and, to repeat the words of President Plimpton of Amherst College at the memorial service following the poet's death: "You never felt you knew a little of Robert Frost and no one ever knew him all.

A dozen years later the poet Archibald MacLeish was saying it this way in the *National Geographic*:
"... it is a sole and single man who speaks, a uniquely singular man .... it is a mistake to look for the New England mind in Frost's work or the New England feel. It was not New England that produced Robert Frost. It was Robert Frost who chose New England."
He also chose Florida.
At first he considered South Florida "a funny land" but as time went on he embraced it with the deep curiousity that was part of his nature. Nothing casual about this man, not ever.
He learned to appreciate the exotic beauty of the rose apple blossom, yet continued to insist that its hollowness made it useless. Here after all, was the man who declared that every regular northern apple should be cut in such a way as to expose a star in its center.
But when I pointed out that the rose apple also made a delicate jelly, he reversed himself.
"Useful," he decided.
To end this book we choose words gleaned from Frost's innumerable public appearances on platforms and from newspaper interviews in his own country and abroad.

"There are too many gangs, cliques, or coteries in poetry. Maybe that's one of the ways they have to manage it. But I'm a lone wolf."

". . . I want poets to be declared equal, I guess to—what shall I say, scientists? No, big business-men. I want poets declared equal to big business-men."

My own favorites are, "People have got to think. Thinking isn't to agree or disagree. That's voting." And, again:

"Ultimately, that is what you go before God for: you've had bad luck and good luck and all you really want in the end is mercy."

Centuries before the American poet was born and named by his father for the General in Chief of the Confederate Armies, General Robert E. Lee, an earlier Bard had been declaring that "the quality of mercy is not strain'd."

William Shakespeare was calling mercy "an attribute to God himself," adding that "earthly power doth then show likest God's when mercy seasons justice."

Justice was clearly the key word in the *New York Times* lead editorial under the heading "Justice Scalia's Poetic License" in its April 22, 1995, issue.

The *Times* was relating how the Frost poem "Mending Wall" had been used as confirmation by Antonin Scalia of the need for constitutional separation of powers. It was in a case involving stock fraud and would have gone unnoticed had it not been for the reference to the Frost poem.

However, Justice Stephen Breyer took the opposite view, i.e. that Frost was declaring *against* walls, rather than *for* them.

This somewhat light-hearted controversy, resulting in a charming *Times* editorial, also elicited a flurry of Letters from readers with opposing views. A fetching sketch of a figure straddling a wall accompanied the Letters.

The whole press event, more than three decades after the agile stirring of the political pot by Robert Frost to gain attention, constituted a cause for celebration.

After the painful character assessments of the poet in the first years following his death, the entire *Times* pieces became a heartening assertion in favor of Robert Frost's continuing effect in this most uncertain world.

Wasn't setting forth several sides of a question and thereby encouraging people to think for themselves part of what he was up to all along?

This is the work of Theodore Spicer-Simson, distinguished medalist, who cast this head of Robert Frost in Coconut Grove.

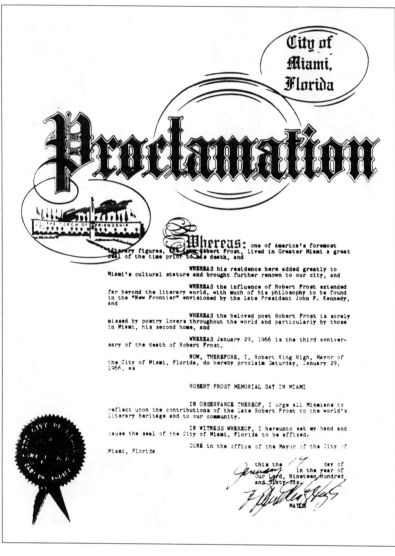

City of
Miami,
Florida

Proclamation

Whereas: one of America's foremost literary figures, the late Robert Frost, lived in Greater Miami a great deal of the time prior to his death, and

WHEREAS his residence here added greatly to Miami's cultural stature and brought further renown to our city, and

WHEREAS the influence of Robert Frost extended far beyond the literary world, with much of his philosophy to be found in the "New Frontier" envisioned by the late President John F. Kennedy, and

WHEREAS the beloved poet Robert Frost is sorely missed by poetry lovers throughout the world and particularly by those in Miami, his second home, and

WHEREAS January 29, 1966 is the third anniversary of the death of Robert Frost,

NOW, THEREFORE, I, Robert King High, Mayor of the City of Miami, Florida, do hereby proclaim Saturday, January 29, 1966, as

ROBERT FROST MEMORIAL DAY IN MIAMI

IN OBSERVANCE THEREOF, I urge all Miamians to reflect upon the contributions of the late Robert Frost to the world's literary heritage and to our community.

IN WITNESS WHEREOF, I hereunto set my hand and cause the seal of the City of Miami, Florida to be affixed.

DONE in the office of the Mayor of the City of Miami, Florida

this the ___ day of _____ in the year of Our Lord, Nineteen Hundred and Sixty-Six.

MAYOR

A proclamation signed by Mayor Robert King High, designating January 29, 1966, as Robert Frost Memorial Day in Miami.

Notes And Acknowledgments

Toward the end of his life Robert Frost urged those interested in publishing his letters, as well as books about him, to wait until he was "good and dead."

Then, in the dedication of his final book, *In The Clearing*, he lifted the ban with these words: "Letters in prose to Louis Untermeyer, Sidney Cox and John Bartlett for them to dispose of as they please; these to you in verse for keeps."

Of all the many books lining the world's bookshelves I have leaned most heavily on one: *Family Letters of Robert and Elinor Frost*, here listed in a Select Bibliography.

It was the greatest assistance in the first two chapters and is recommended for anyone interested in Robert Frost, the person.

That collection of letters, together with my own journals, supplied me with much of what I needed to provide material for this view of the poet, which is obviously the years spent in the State of Florida and particularly in Miami where we became friends.

It is not uncomplicated to sift through the wealth of scholarly material relating to such a dramatic literary figure, and the cooperation of others is a necessity.

The name Lawrance Thompson, Frost's hand-picked biographer, has been mentioned in the Introduction and elsewhere in this book in connection with the stir caused by the publication of his biographies, particularly the second.

It should be said here and now that Thompson, while presenting a faulty picture of Frost, does at the same time offer a body of information about events in the poet's entire life and therefore I have listed them under the Bibliography and used them to corroborate certain events.

My own library holds a sizable collection of books on Frost as well as various periodicals and some will be listed as well.

It goes without saying that I received assistance from Florida libraries beginning with Joan Morris, Archives, Florida State Library and Sam Boldrick, manager of the Miami-Dade Public Library Florida Room and from Director Mary Somerville and Executive Secretary Maurice Elam, who all provided courtesies.

Over and over I consulted with William E. Brown, Jr., head, Archives and Special Collections, Richter Library, University of Miami and with Director Frank Rodgers.

Sam Boldrick steered me toward Kathleen J. Reich, associate professor, Archives, Rollins College, who made available manuscript letters from Robert Frost contained in the Jessie B. Rittenhouse Collection in the Mills Library.

Included in the general collection is a first edition of *North of Boston* and inscribed by the poet.

While he never visited the campus, Frost was given a party at the home of Mr. and Mrs. Robert Lamont of Oviedo at which time the vice president of Rollins, Dr. A.J. Hanna, brought some of the Rittenhouse exhibits over to show to the poet.

Frost assured him that the volume was worth between two hundred and three hundred dollars and signed the book with these words: "So Jessie had this very first of my English books! Expressing my pleased surprise this late in the day—March 11, 1957."

Charles E. Miller, director of libraries of Florida State University, reported that Robert Frost was slated to speak on March 22, 1938, but was prevented by the death of his wife. *The Flambeau*, a student newspaper, announced the cancellation.

A later appearance was on February 6, 1941, at an American Association of University Women Lecture Series and photographs of the event were provided to us.

Director Randy F. Nimnicht and Becky Smith were ready with help at the Historical Association of Southern Florida Museum, and Trammell Lonas of Alexandria, Virginia, researched certain materials in the nation's capital, while Dorothea Ellison did the same in San Antonio, Texas.

Martha Coolidge shared memories of her childhood in Brewster Village where Robert Frost moved after his wife's death in order to establish a Cambridge, Massachusetts base, and Bertram Zuckerman, of the Fairchild Tropical Garden Research Center, provided photographs.

The recollections of Hervey Allen's children and of Nettie Belle Hjort Robinson, who grew up close by Robert Frost at *Pencil Pines*, were invaluable.

Marcia Allen, Mary Ann Marcus and Richard Allen all contributed. The latter, a professor at the University of California at Berkeley and the author of *Fire And Iron: Critical Approaches to Njáls Saga* (University of Pittsburgh), supplied original unpublished material relating to the death of Elinor Frost in Florida and his father's role with the poet immediately after in 1938. All of this was much appreciated by me.

I consulted over and over with Marcia Allen and Nettie Belle Hjort Robinson, and with George W. Rosner, retired archivist librarian of the University of Miami, who lived next door to Robert Frost for a number of years. He steered me toward Dr. Robert Read, who occupied one of the Frost cottages for a brief period at the end of the poet's life.

I appreciate the assistance of Dr. Franz H. Stewart, Sr., in obtaining the precise medical report of Robert Frost's serious illness in 1962 in Miami, and for that extended by Martha Magruder O'Brien in making available the entire file of letters exchanged with her mother, the late Martha Magruder, in the course of Robert Frost's purchase of *Pencil Pines* during which she served as real estate agent.

The enthusiastic response by Bill Prahl to the request for information concerning the construction of the fireplace late in the poet's life was a help in forming a picture of Robert Frost's own response to the people of

South Florida as were the warm recollections of Dr. Read and Bea Moss, both of whom lived in one of the cottages at different times.

To these and those others, who when they heard that I was embarked on this piece of work, offered encouragement, goes my gratitude. This includes dear friends like writer Karen Pryor, daughter of Philip Wylie, and Wini and John Hawkes of Dorset, Vermont. Nettie Belle and John Robinson went so far as to join with me in attempting to describe the exact shade of blue for Robert Frost's eyes.

We went from "sky blue" to "electric" until I decided to use "arresting" blue eyes. I did so on the grounds that Robert Frost would have leaned more in that direction, knowing full well that the entire idea would have amused him no end.

My warm thanks go to Joyce Carol Oates for allowing me to use the quotation in the front of this book. It comes from *Foxfire* and served to spur me on in the writing of *Frost in Florida*.

I am grateful for the conversations I held with both Robert Frost's granddaughters, Elinor Wilber and Lesley Lee Francis, and with Anne Morrison Smyth and Edward Connery Lathem, as well as my own daughter, Mary Burrell.

A happy addition to the numbers of words written about Frost occurred while I was writing this book when *The Frost Family's Adventure in Poetry, Sheer Morning Gladness at the Brim*, was published by the University of Missouri. It is a meticulous account of the period in England by Lesley Lee Francis and constitutes an ap-

propriate family contribution to the life of Robert Lee
Frost, Poet.

Finally, a salute to editor Mark Seibel who took the
view that this book would be more valuable as a mem-
oir than a less personal account and patiently and repeatedly pointed it out.

Select Bibliography

Anderson, Margaret Bartlett, *Robert Frost and John Bartlett, The Record of a Friendship,* Holt Rinehart Winston, 1963.

Bain, David Howard and Mary Smyth Duffy, ed. *Whose Woods These Are, A History of the Bread Loaf Writers' Conference 1926-1992,* The Ecco Press, 1993.

Brodsky, Joseph, "Close Readings: On Grief and Reason," *The New Yorker,* September 26, 1994.

Burnshaw, Stanley, *Robert Frost Himself,* New York: George Braziller, 1986.

Clark, Ida M., "Building a Home for Frost," *Update,* Vol. 12, No.1, The Historical Association of Southern Florida, February 1985.

Cohen, Edward H., "Robert Frost in England: An Unpublished Letter," *The New England Quarterly,* Vol. XLIII, No. 2, June 1970.

176

Francis, Lesley Lee, *The Frost Family's Adventure in Poetry, Sheer Morning Gladness at the Brim,* University of Missouri Press, 1994.

Frost, Lesley, "Certain Intensities," *Forum,* Vol. XV, No. 3, Ball State University, Summer 1974.

Frost, Robert, "Before the Beginning and After the End of a Poem," *The Carrell,* Journal of the Friends of the University of Miami Library, Vol. 6, No. 2, December 1965.

Gordon, Marie, "Robert Frost at Home," *The Carrell,* Journal of the Friends of the University of Miami Library, Vol. 17, 1976.

Grade, Arnold, ed. *Family Letters of Robert and Elinor Frost,* Albany: University of New York Press, 1978.

Jerome, Judson, *A Tribute To Robert Frost, Writer's Digest,* April 1963.

Koch, Frederick H. "Robert Frost at Seventy-five," *The Carrell,* Journal of the Friends of the University of Miami Library, Vol. 17, 1976.

Lathem, Edward Connery, ed., *Interviews With Robert Frost,* Holt Rinehart Winston, 1966.

Lathem, Edward Connery and Lawrance Thompson, ed., *Robert Frost: Farm-Poultryman*, Dartmouth Publications, 1963.

The Letters of Robert Frost to Louis Untermeyer, Holt Rinehart Winston, 1963.

Monroe, Harriet and Alice Corbin Henderson, ed., *The New Poetry: An Anthology*, The Macmillan Company, 1920.

Morrison, Kathleen, *Robert Frost, A Pictorial Chronicle*, Holt Rinehart Winston, 1974.

Poirier, Richard, *Robert Frost, The Work of Knowing*, Oxford University Press, 1977.

Pritchard, William H., *Frost, A Literary Life Reconsidered*, Oxford University Press, 1984.

Richards, Norman, "Robert Frost's New England," *United Air Lines Mainliner*, December 1968.

Robinson, Nettie Belle Hjort, "My Neighbor Mr. Frost," *Update*, Vol. 4, No. 2, Historical Association of Southern Florida, December 1976.

Rosner, George W., "Robert Frost at the University of Miami," *The Carrell*, Journal of the Friends of the University of Miami Library, Vol. 17, 1976.

Sergeant, Elizabeth Shepley, *Robert Frost: The Trial by Existence*, Holt, Rinehart Winston, 1960.

Stegner, Wallace, *The Uneasy Chair, A Biography of Bernard DeVoto*, Doubleday and Company, Inc., 1974.

Thompson, Lawrance, *Selected Letters of Robert Frost*, Holt Rinehart Winston, 1964.

———— *Robert Frost: The Early Years, 1874-1915*, Holt, Rinehart Winston, 1966.

———— *Robert Frost: The Years of Triumph, 1915-1938*, Holt Rinehart Winston, 1970.

Thompson, Lawrance, and Arnold Grade, comps. *New Hampshire's Child, The Derry Journals of Lesley Frost*, Albany: State University of New York Press, 1969.

Thompson, Lawrance, and R.H. Winnick, *Robert Frost, The Later Years, 1938-1963*, Holt Rinehart Winston, 1976.

Walsh, John Evangelist, *Into My Own, The English Years of Robert Frost*, 1912-1915, Grove Press, 1988.

PERMISSIONS

Photo Credits: Front Cover and pp. 53, 117, 126, — (courtesy Dartmouth College Library); p. xi—Tim Chapman, (courtesy *The Miami Herald*); p. 11—(courtesy the City of Coral Gables); p. 31 —(courtesy Marcia A. Allen); p. 48—(courtesy Robert Manning Strozier Library, Florida State University, Tallahassee, Florida); p. 55—(courtesy Mal Ferrell); p. 59—(courtesy Karen Pryor); p. 66—Fred Fleming, (courtesy Marcia A. Allen); p. 70—(courtesy Archives at the Special Collections, Fairchild Tropical Garden); Back Cover—Masud Quraishy and pp. 89, 91, 93, 167, 168—(courtesy Helen Muir); p. 90—(courtesy Archives in Special Collections at Middlebury College, Middlebury, Vermont); pp. 115, 118—(courtesy Archives and Special Collections Department, Otto G. Richter Library, University of Miami, Coral Gables, Florida); p.122—Johnston Photography Collection (courtesy University of Florida Archives); p. 123—Fred A. Chapman (courtesy University of Florida Archives); p. 127—(courtesy Jeane Porter, Jessie Porter's Heritage House Museum, Key West, Florida); p. 130—(courtesy University of Miami Photo Center); p. 159—(courtesy Lesley Lee Francis).

180

INDEX